MODERN ESSAYS

MODERN ESSAYS

REPRINTED FROM LEADING
ARTICLES IN "THE TIMES"

WITH AN INTRODUCTION BY

J W. MACKAIL

FELLOW OF THE ROYAL SOCIETY OF LITERATURE

Essay Index Reprint Series

BOOKS FOR LIBRARIES PRESS
FREEPORT, NEW YORK

First Published 1915
Reprinted 1970

STANDARD BOOK NUMBER:
8369-1630-1

LIBRARY OF CONGRESS CATALOG CARD NUMBER:
73-86788

PRINTED IN THE UNITED STATES OF AMERICA

CONTENTS

		PAGE
INTRODUCTION	. . . .	ix
THE WISDOM OF THE AGES	. . . .	1
THE SECRET OF SUCCESS	. . . . .	4
THE ORDINARY MAN	. . . . .	8
PRIGGISHNESS	. . . .	12
THE COWARDICE OF YOUTH	. . . .	17
CHARLATANS	. . . . . .	20
ON FRIENDSHIP	. . . . . .	24
ON UNDERSTANDING OTHERS	. . . .	27
COLLECTORS	. . . .	31
ON GIVING ADVICE	. . . . . .	35
CURIOSITY	. . . .	38
UGLINESS	. . . .	41
MORAL INDIGNATION	. . . . . .	45
PARADOX	. . . .	49
RESPECTABILITY	. . . . . .	52
ON BEING A GENTLEMAN	. . . . .	56
CHILDISHNESS	. . . .	60
MEANNESS AND ITS MOTIVE	. . . .	63
ANTICIPATION AND MEMORY	. . . .	66
DIFFERENCES OF TASTE	. . . . .	69

v

Modern Essays

	PAGE
BAD TASTE IN CONDUCT	73
TASTE AND ITS STANDARDS	77
MIND AND CIRCUMSTANCE	82
THE LATIN GENIUS	86
THREATENING LETTERS AND WITCHCRAFT	90
SHYNESS AND HATRED	93
THE VICTORIAN AGE	97
THE EFFICIENT MANNER	101
GRUMBLING	105
THE FUTURE OF KNOWLEDGE	109
PLEASURE AND COMFORT	113
"THE LAW OF PROGRESS"	116
LIVING IN THE PAST	121
MUTUAL ADMIRATION SOCIETIES	125
WHAT MIGHT HAVE BEEN	129
THE PERSPECTIVE OF LIFE	134
PRACTICAL JOKES	138
IDEALISM OF OUR TIME	141
BY-PRODUCTS	145
RHYTHM AND PURPOSE	149
TAKE NO THOUGHT FOR YESTERDAY	152
THE ASCETIC	155
PHILOSOPHY AND POETRY	158
THE SURVIVAL OF SUPERSTITION	162
THE FEAR OF THE INFINITE	165
THE EGOTIST	169
UNORTHODOXY	173

Contents

		PAGE
ORTHODOXY	. . . .	177
THE CRAVING FOR SOLITUDE	. . . .	180
TWO KINDS OF OPTIMISM	. . . . .	185
CYNICISM OLD AND NEW	. . . . .	188
THE PLAIN MAN	. . . . . .	191
AMATEUR AND PROFESSIONAL	. . . .	195
MYTHS ANCIENT AND MODERN	. . . .	198
CASTLES IN THE AIR	. . . . . .	202
" I TOLD YOU SO "	. . . . . .	205
BOOKS IN WAR-TIME	. . . . . .	209
ON TABOOS	. . . . . .	212
THE LOVE OF MONEY	. . . .	215
NAUGHTINESS	. . . . . .	219
THE KNOWING MAN	. . . . . .	223
TWO KINDS OF FAMILY FEELING	. . .	227
THE SILLY SEASON	. . . . . .	230
HOLIDAYS NEW AND OLD	. . . . .	234
GOOD FRIDAY	. . . . . .	238
HASTE AND WASTE	. . . . . .	241
VISIONS OF NIGHT	. . . . . .	244
THE SEASIDE	. . . . . .	246
THE COMING OF SPRING	. . . . .	251
THE TEMPERANCE OF SPRING	. . . .	254
BEAUTY AND DESTRUCTION	. . . .	257
MAN AND NATURE	. . . . . .	259
HORSE-CHESTNUT BUDS	. . . . .	262
LIFE IN THE WIND	. . . . . .	264

Modern Essays

	PAGE
LENT LILIES	267
ON COLOUR	269
"NATURE"	273
A MORAL FROM BLACKBEETLES	276
THE ROD AND THE CHILD	279
CHILDREN IN WAR-TIME	282
LEARNERS AND TEACHERS	286
SCHOOLMASTERS OLD AND NEW	289

INTRODUCTION

No apology is required for the collection of these essays in a more permanent form. Nor perhaps, it may be said, can any necessity for an introduction be claimed. For such an introduction is, in fact, but adding to them one essay more. As Pembroke says to King John :

> "This once again, but that your highness pleas'd,
> Was once superfluous."

But to follow a courteous usage need not be regarded as " wasteful and ridiculous excess."

The type of leading article represented here is a feature not common to many newspapers, and is honourable to journalism. For it adds to the scope of journalism, and attaches to it a higher, perhaps a not less useful, function. The ordinary leading article deals with public affairs of the moment, or with current incidents and controversies. It gathers up and comments on the news which is the staple content of the newspaper as such. But, like the news of the day, the daily comment on it is transitory and soon forgotten. One thinks as little of re-reading yesterday's leading article as of re-reading yesterday's news. To-day has come, with its fresh news and the fresh reflections made upon it. Both have for the moment a paramount value; they are that for which the newspaper exists, and for which we read it. The news of the day and the daily comment made on it give necessary information, and help (or are supposed to help) to interpret it to us. Between them, they rouse feeling and suggest action, as well as keeping us in touch with the daily movement of the world ; but they do not satisfy the intelligence, nor except indirectly do they enlarge the mind, or lead it towards the real realities. Those who read nothing but newspapers—how many !—are starving their minds ; and the starvation is none the less real for those who gorge themselves with this food.

The " third leaders " in *The Times* of which this volume is a selection are meant to supplement this deficiency. They are meant to turn the reader from affairs and interests of the moment to a consideration " of man, of nature, and of human life " in their larger, more permanent aspect. They may still deal, not indeed with events, but with fashions or tendencies, theories or experiences, of the immediate present. But even with these they deal in a more detached way, from a wider point of view. Oftener still they are concerned with things that have a more true permanence ; with the elements of human nature, the springs of action, the problems of life and conduct ; with the effective meaning of art or of science ; with the recurrent and perpetual pageant of the visible world. In one or another form, they represent the daily demand and supply of material for thought. Their value, whether great or small, is not for one day only, ceasing with the next. It is right then and reasonable that the more valuable of them should be preserved and collected. They are journalism ; but

Introduction

in them journalism is extending itself towards, is even becoming, literature.

Such a collection is not in any sense a single work of art; it is hardly, except in a purely mechanical sense, a book. It has no structure or continuity. Its parts have no relation beyond the slight element of connexion or contrast which may be given them by skilful arrangement. Nor is it meant to be (if indeed it can be) read continuously, any more than a hymn-book. It is a volume to take up and to lay down on occasion, for pleasure; and for profit.

The mention of a hymn-book may recall the celebrated passage in John Wesley's Preface to his own and his brother's hymns. The authors of this collection might perhaps have deputed one of their own number to introduce it in words taken textually, with the substitution of *essays* for *hymns*, from that priceless apologia. "I will speak to those who are judges, with all freedom and unreserve. To these I may say without offence: 1. In these essays there is no doggerel; no botches; nothing put in to patch up; no feeble expletives. 2. Here is nothing turgid nor bombast on the one hand, or low and creeping on the other. 3. Here are no *cant* expressions; no words without meaning. Those who impute this to us know not what they say. We talk common sense, and use no word but in a fixed determinate sense. 4. Here are, allow me to say, both the purity, the strength, and the elegance of the English language, and, at the same time, the utmost simplicity and plainness, suited to every capacity." That fearless old fashion is, unhappily, out of date.

Modern Essays

To read these essays on end may not be impossible, but certainly would be undesirable. Not only would there be found in them some amount of repetition; but the similarity of treatment imposed by their conformity to a recognised if not prescribed journalistic type would necessarily give them, quite unjustly, an effect of monotony. Notwithstanding variety of authorship, notwithstanding distinctions (as well as distinction) of style, the mould in which they are cast was determined beforehand. And their collection thus side by side lays the device—shall we be so bold as to say the trick?—of their construction open to sight, and perhaps to a somewhat amused criticism. Under such a test, the mechanism is apt to become a little too obvious, the verbal adroitness and deft manipulation of thought may seem to be those of a game played for its own sake, and the free play of intelligence to be exercised as much over the ways of expressing ideas as over the ideas themselves. Canon Scott Holland, whose jocundity has never any touch of malice, has poked some quiet fun in his own collected volume of biographical essays, *A Bundle of Memories*, at what he calls "the skilled gentry of the *Times Literary Supplement*." Perhaps he would accept for them a phrase which occurs in an essay in this volume as not undescriptive, "early birds with a power of expressing their own satisfaction in the form of a theory." But there is no reproach in good craftsmanship, and no discredit in being concerned with ideas as well as with persons, with what makes our lives as well as with lives actually made. Both go to make up the fabric of the world.

Introduction

The essay, not only in its chosen ground of the eighteenth century, but ever since it became a recognised literary form, has been more popular than most of its competitors. Partly this is because (as Mr. Oldbuck suggested to Lovel about blank verse as against rhyme) it is easier to write; partly because it satisfies the desire of handling ideas and yet not undergoing any severe or prolonged mental strain; but mainly because as a medium it is so flexible, so accommodating and various. Between the type of Montaigne and the type of Bacon there is room to expatiate as widely as heart could desire. On the one hand there is the essay of distilled thought, concentrated experience, pregnant language; on the other, the essay which lets itself drift from point to point, following casual links of suggestion, thinking aloud, and stopping not because there is no more to say, but because the writer must somewhere lay down his pen. But for the origin of the essay as a dominant type, we must go back beyond Bacon or Montaigne, to a work which had in its time a much larger European reputation than either. The *Adagia* of Erasmus was the most widely read book of the early sixteenth century. It was the gospel of humanism, diluted and expanded for popular consumption. The authors of these essays are also, in their way, keeping up the humanistic tradition. They have not been, as Erasmus was, taken away before the evil to come, before Europe was drenched in blood and the hopes of a century extinguished. But neither is the new humanism defeated or dead.

From the *Adagia* of Erasmus to the *Exagia*, the

Modern Essays

Essais, of Montaigne, is a far journey; yet the similarity of the two words is curious. By etymology they have no connexion whatever; by accident they took an equated form; and the substance of what they meant came to be much the same. Both are *sermones*, in the Latin sense; discourses or discussions, starting from some title—a proverb, an aphorism, a popular phrase, perhaps merely a word of common use—and examining it, expanding it and bringing out its implications, putting it into relation with thought, with principles, with experience. In Bacon (*Essays or Counsels Civil and Moral* is his full title) the essay is marked not only by studied brevity but by the " arduous fulness " named by Rossetti as the note of the sonnet. But more commonly, both essay and sonnet are vehicles for noting down and interpreting incidents and impressions, for excursions of thought and adventures of fancy. *Saggi morali*, the title given to the Italian translation of Bacon's Essays, well describes some of the pieces in the present volume, like those on Friendship, on Philosophy and Poetry, on the Future of Knowledge, on Man and Nature. Others, like those on Differences of Taste, or on Castles in the Air, are " colours of good and evil," studies in the byways of human nature. And others again, like the two beautiful studies entitled " The Coming of Spring " and " Life in the Wind," are æsthetic and imaginative interpretations of external nature. All of them are the easy talk of educated and receptive minds, quick to follow and apt to convey suggestions; with a skilled touch in discourse which makes listening pleasant, while yet it stimulates the listener's

xiv

Introduction

own active thought. This suggestiveness is their primary merit, while a certain preciosity (this is, I suppose, what Canon Scott Holland feels when he speaks with indulgent humour of skilled gentry) is the risk that lurks for them round the corner.

All art is personal. In some of these studies we may seem to trace the attitude of a middle-age which has just realised itself and has begun to have a consuming interest in youth. To this stage of life belong the wistful and only half-convinced reflections on the gains that age brings. A little further forward, we cease to think much about loss or gain, and life becomes more of a single thing. In the essay on Mind and Circumstance this point is well taken. " Self-forgetfulness is the best possible habit for the mind to acquire. Indeed if we can acquire it, so as to maintain it through all changes of circumstance, we have learnt the secret of life. Happiness, as opposed to occasional and precarious joys, consists in this active power." But those who have found this happiness do not speak of it, they hardly think of it. Perhaps the matter was put in a nutshell by that lady, of great experience of life and remarkable insight, who began a sentence in conversation with the words " As I grow older and less wise."

It is part, and not the least part, of the suggestiveness of these essays that they not merely stimulate thought, but often do so by rousing question or dissent. " The middle-aged man knows what he wants " ; rather surely, he knows what he does not want, which is far from being the same thing. " To state it (the conviction of a philosopher) barely is not

to state it at all "; the propounder of this aphorism
must settle matters himself with Aristotle and Spinoza.
Exceptions like these may be taken to a score of
passages; and this is what gives the essays so much
interest and vitality. They make one think, doubt,
oppose: one talks back to the voice that talks in
them, and mind stirs against mind.

At a time like the present it is more important than
ever to keep the mind open, and to keep it steady.
Equanimity, the dying watchword of the Roman
Emperor who was emphatically surnamed the Good,
means something far more than acquiescence, far
higher than resignation. It means the spirit which
refuses to be fretted or narrowed, which makes a
delight and not merely a service of duty, which knows
that life has still joy, and that joy carries with it
strength, fitness, usefulness. These writers may be
reckoned as also in some sense sharers, far away from
the firing-line and the munition factory, in the work
of upholding the complex fabric of civilisation against
the greatest strain it has ever had to meet. For to
stir intelligence and to kindle interest in man and
nature not only relieves but strengthens, not only
sweetens but enlarges life.

J. W. MACKAIL.

MODERN ESSAYS

THE WISDOM OF THE AGES

WHEN we are young we do not believe enough in the wisdom of the ages, and when we are old we believe too much in it. At both stages we fail to discriminate, and there are few who acquire that further individual wisdom which can tell when the wisdom of the ages is really wise and when it is merely a solemn substitute for necessary thought. We must never expect any man to show the wisdom of the ages where his own interests or passions are concerned; that wisdom is always advice given by the indifferent world to the interested individual, and the problem for the interested individual is to know when the world can advise him better than he can advise himself. He will be wrong if he never takes its advice, and he will be wrong if he always takes it; but he must not trust his own feelings about it, for if he does that he will only take it when it is agreeable to those feelings.

There is a kind of man who goes about seeking advice until he gets the advice he wants. He knows, at the back of his mind, what he will do from the first. It is not advice that he really seeks, but some one to confirm him in doing what he wishes to do.

A

He has no principle in accepting or rejecting the wisdom of the ages ; and it is a principle that we need to tell us when the general opinion is likely to be wiser than the opinion of the wisest individual. This general opinion is always of necessity a generalisation. The individual knows the particular circumstances of his case better than anyone else ; and therefore a generalisation is likely to be of use to him only when his particular knowledge is perverted by particular feeling. As a rule, for instance, each of us knows what he wants better than anyone else. Thus, when we are choosing a house, we do not, if we are wise, look to the general opinion to tell us what we want. But, knowing what we want, we may consult an expert as to the best means of getting it. His is not the wisdom of the ages, but merely superior knowledge applied to detail, and it is that knowledge, not wisdom, that we ask of him.

In most of the affairs of life, then, we must not look to the wisdom of the ages to tell us what we want ; for on that point the wisdom of the ages becomes merely vague platitude or conventional timidity. But there are times when we are so disturbed by passion that we do not know ourselves what we really want— when, for instance, the itch for revenge is so urgent that our reason will only work to provide pretexts for it. In such cases all our special knowledge has turned to feeling. The more we know about our own wrongs, the more we feel that they are not to be endured. Then is the time to go to some one who knows little about our wrongs and cares less. Any sensible man can apply the wisdom of the ages to a wounded egotism, just as any one can warn a man with a raging thirst not to drink from a tainted stream. It is not that the man who gives the warning is wiser, but that he has not a raging thirst. The world does know by ages of experience that the pleasure of revenge is seldom worth having, and that the man who wants it wants it usually only with his wounded egotism, not with his whole nature, which for the time is put out of action by the one appetite for revenge. And the injured man himself, if he seeks advice, knows this too in his heart. He seeks it because he needs some outside help against the tyranny of his own egotism, because he wants to be told very gently but firmly that he is a fool, because he wishes some one else to provide him with arguments that he is too weak to provide for himself.

In such cases the wisdom of the ages is merely what every sensible man knows when he is not provoked into folly ; and every sensible man, even when he is provoked to folly, can recognise that wisdom. But there is another kind of traditional wisdom, based upon long experience, which it is more difficult to distinguish from traditional platitude. There is, for instance, a great deal of traditional wisdom concerned with falling in love and with married life which the lover or the young husband is apt to despise because he cannot believe that any one has ever been really in love before. But it is just because so many men and women have been in love, because love is the one high and passionate adventure common to mankind

3

that they have produced a traditional wisdom about it unlike all their other traditional wisdom.

Most of our proverbs are cautious ; they tell us in a hundred different ways how all that glitters is not gold. But the proverbs concerned with love do not say that. They say that faint heart never won fair lady, and that all is fair in love and war. True, there is one about marrying in haste and repenting at leisure ; but that sounds rather like an argument for the reform of the divorce laws than a warning against love. Every man who has married for love is a little proud that he was bold enough to do so ; and his boldness in this one adventure of the spirit has made him think boldly for once. So, about love, we have an adventurous philosophy which is wiser than all the exaltations and misgivings of the individual lover. The world knows that men are always falling in love, but he thinks that he is feeling what no man ever felt before, and he is often afraid of the unprecedented symptoms of his own passion. In this case the world tells him not to be afraid, and there it is like the high sages who tell us not to be afraid of death. Its wisdom about love comes from love, and that is the reason why it is wise.

THE SECRET OF SUCCESS

MR. ROOSEVELT once divided success into two kinds : the rare kind which comes to the man who can do what no one else can do, to the genius ; and the commoner

kind, which comes to the man who has developed
ordinary qualities further than most men. This distinction would be difficult to draw in practice. There
can be no doubt that the genius of Mozart included
special powers which in the ordinary man are not only
undeveloped, but also non-existent. But Napoleon
also was a genius ; and we cannot say that any of
his powers do not exist in the ordinary man. His
genius, and even his almost magical influence over
men, were only the result of an extraordinary combina-
tion and development of ordinary powers. We cannot
say that he had a special faculty such as we find in
great artists ; and, indeed, Emerson, in his studies
of Representative Men, took Napoleon as the man
of the world, seeming therefore to insist upon the
fact that his genius consisted only of ordinary qualities
very highly developed. Again, men are often born
with a very wonderful special faculty, whether for
musical composition or chess-playing or mathematics,
whom no one would call men of genius. The technical
gift of Mozart is not very uncommon ; but we do
not call it genius unless it is combined with the less
specialised and less easily defined power of using it
to express something of moment. Such gifts are
mere tools, whose value depends upon the manner
in which they are used, although the man who does
not possess them must be continually hampered
by the lack of them. But Mr. Roosevelt, who
was addressing an audience mainly consisting of
ordinary men, was inclined to insist upon the fact
that success in most things can be obtained with-

out these extraordinary gifts. He took the line of
Reynolds, who, in addressing the students of the
Academy, almost contended that there was no
such thing as genius even in painting, and that
a man of ordinary gifts could reach the highest
excellence in it by a right and assiduous use of his
powers.

Here we are not far from the idea that genius consists in taking pains. But, when we say that the
right kind of pains must always be taken, we leave
genius a good deal of its mystery. For one of the
main difficulties in every activity, whether art or
statesmanship or science or business, is to take the
right kind of pains, to attempt what is best suited to
the powers of the individual and also to the object
he has in view. There is a kind of sagacity needed
for this which we cannot analyse, and for the lack of
which the most splendid natural gifts are often wasted.
Thus, when Mr. Roosevelt tells us that for great
success all we need is the extraordinary development
of ordinary qualities, he still leaves us in the dark
about that power which some men possess of develop-
ing ordinary qualities into an extraordinary efficiency
for a particular purpose. There is a secret of success
which he has not analysed, and which we do not
explain when we call it will or energy or character
or common sense. It is not merely will or energy,
because there is in it a power of direction which these
words do not imply. Character is a word too vague,
and used in too many different senses, to explain
anything; and as for common sense, the very fact

that it is common prevents it from being the cause of uncommon success.

In men who succeed greatly, whether we call them men of genius or not, there is often an urgency of desire not to be found in the great mass of mankind. They seem to know very clearly what they want to do, and from the first employ all their powers in doing it. By a kind of instinct they plan their lives so that no effort of theirs is wasted, and so that all their experience and actions have a cumulative power; and this is the case whether their success is material or spiritual or scientific or artistic. When we read the lives of great men we cannot but be struck by the manner in which all kinds of experiences that might in themselves seem to be random, or even disastrous, are utilised in the long run.

There are saints who would never have attained to such a height and subtlety of virtue if they had not been sinners· in their youth. There are artists who, through early hack work, obtain a peculiar pliancy and swiftness of accomplishment. There are statesmen who seem to learn all that they need to know about men in a quiet country life. Such were Saint Augustine, Shakespeare, and Cromwell—all as different from each other as any men could be, yet having in common the mysterious and most valuable power of profiting by every kind of experience. Cromwell, indeed, seems to have become a statesman and general only because the emergency called for him. But for the Civil War he might have been a country gentleman all his life. And yet he must have been learning from the first, and from all his quite ordinary experiences, lessons such as most men never learn at all. In fact, he must have had that mental power of digestion which is the main secret of success even in those activities which also need very special gifts, the power which made Rembrandt a greater painter than Vandyck, Beethoven a greater composer than Mendelssohn, Shakespeare a greater poet than Fletcher; which, wherever it is used, always sets the master far above the mere brilliant specialist.

THE ORDINARY MAN

MR. BALFOUR has said that there ought not to be a different law for the picturesque and the commonplace any more than for the rich and the poor. He was speaking of the criminal law; but we may give his words a wider application. There are many people now who exult in their freedom from the older kinds of snobbery, who worship neither rank nor wealth, but who make a snobbish distinction between the distinguished and the commonplace, and talk contemptuously of the ordinary man as if he were a mere super in the play of life. Indeed, they regard life as a play acted for their amusement. Distinguished people for them are the star actors in it, admired because they have the gift of expression, because they can dominate a scene and manifest a clear intention in all that they say and do. It is a great

gift, but the fact remains that life is not a play. There
are no supers in it and, among men, no spectators
with the spectator's right of criticism. Directly we
regard ourselves as spectators, we assume the position
of gods and put ourselves in a false relation with
the whole of life. We forget, in our contempt of the
ordinary man, that we ourselves are liable to be re
garded not as spectators, but as actors, and to be
condemned also as ordinary. When we despise the
crowd of supers, we despise ourselves ; and when we
question their right to exist, we question our own.
But no man thinks of himself as a super in life or
questions his own right to exist, unless his mind is
sick. No man is ordinary to himself ; for every one
has at least enough self-knowledge to know that he
is an individual different in a thousand respects from
other men. Only ignorance could regard him as one
of a herd, or classify him as a type. Therefore he
should assume a like ignorance in himself when he is
tempted to think of other men as ordinary.

There is a common fashion nowadays of classifying
men as if they were animals or plants, which is supposed to be scientific. It is not knowledge, but the
lack of it, that produces these classifications. To the
hasty European all Chinamen look alike. That is
because he thinks of them not as men, but as Chinamen. He has only one kind of relation to them,
which is entirely negative. They are to him merely
not Europeans. So to the complete egotist, if there
were such a man, all other men would be merely not
himself.

Modern Essays

It is this kind of negative relation, based upon ignorance and lack of interest, that makes us think of whole multitudes of men as ordinary, and causes us to resent their supposed uniformity. If we go about the world expecting to be amused, and judging mankind by their power of amusing us, we are naturally led to condemn all who do not amuse us as commonplace. But the proper business of mankind is not to amuse us. We have no right to expect a pleasant and passive experience of life. We can only attain to wisdom and knowledge by an active experience of it, and by entering into active relations with other men. Directly we do that, we find that all men are individuals like ourselves, not to be classified any more than we are to be classified, but each one having his own secrets of character, his own peculiar reaction against circumstance, his own process of growth and decay. The saying that no man is a hero to his valet is supposed to be cynical; but there is a truth in it that is not cynical. Every man, to those who know him closely, cannot be described by any title or label. The hero is something besides a hero, just as the ordinary man is something more than an ordinary man. He is himself, with an identity that cannot be described in terms of mere praise or blame; and those who have intimate relations with him are more aware of this identity than of any general effect produced by his public actions.

The greatest masters of drama and fiction, such as Tolstoy and Shakespeare, seldom present their characters to us in terms of praise or blame, nor do they make us feel that some of them are ordinary and some distinguished. For them there is not one law for the picturesque and another for the commonplace. They are interested in men because they are men, and their curiosity about humanity is insatiable and disinterested. They seem to have a boundless power of creation, because they do not classify men according to some narrow or negative relation of their own with them. We feel that they have not gone about the world expecting to be amused, that their experience of mankind has been active, not passive, that they understand men because they have seen each one of them from his own point of view and by that means learned the secrets of his identity.

The chief weakness of lesser writers is that they classify according to some system in vogue at their time. Some divide men sharply into good and bad; others into gentle and simple. Our present novelists are very apt to insist upon the difference between the distinguished and the commonplace. If one of their characters is distinguished, he may do, with the applause of the writer, what he pleases. If he is commonplace, he can do nothing that is not ridiculous. The very words " distinguished " and " distinction," so often used now, betray the nature of our classifications. We praise a man because he has evident points of difference from other men, because he catches the eye in a crowd and seems an exception to a wearisome uniformity. But it is the business of a master of fiction to see distinctions where they are not forced upon him; and, if he condemns any man as ordinary, he condemns himself for his own lack of observation. The Christian doctrine that every man has an immortal soul has an artistic as well as a moral importance. The writer who believes it more than conventionally will feel that he is concerned with the immortal souls of all his characters; and he will realise that, when he presents a character as merely commonplace, he is only betraying the fact that he has not discovered his immortal soul, which is the one thing worth discovering about him.

So it is with all of us when we find ourselves wearied with the uniformity of man. We are wearied with a delusion produced not by the delicacy of our perceptions, but by their bluntness. Some men have more power of expressing themselves than others, and men of genius express themselves in all that they do or say. But the lack of expressive power does not mean that there is nothing to be expressed. Every man is aware that there is a great deal worth expressing in himself, and he may be sure that he knows himself better than he knows others.

PRIGGISHNESS

PRIGGISHNESS is one of those minor vices which provoke more dislike than many greater ones; and prig is a favourite term of abuse, because it is wounding without being libellous. A man has his remedy against

anyone who calls him a thief, and he can prove that
he is not one in a court of law ; but he cannot prove
that he is not a prig. Indeed, his very efforts to
prove it may arouse further suspicion against him.
If he were not a prig, we think, he would only smile
at the accusation, as a humorous man would only
smile at the accusation that he has no sense of humour.

In all highly civilised societies the social virtues are
the most esteemed and the social vices are the most
condemned ; and priggishness is a social vice. A prig
cannot talk about the weather without betraying the
fact that he is a prig ; or, rather, he will probably
proclaim his priggishness by refusing to talk about
the weather on principle. We all know that the
weather is not a topic likely to produce brilliant conversation, but we choose it as an opening, a gambit ;
and there is both wisdom and politeness in the choice.
For the weather may lead to anything ; conversation
will grow out of it naturally, and neither party will
force his own subject on the other. But the prig
wants to force his own subject ; he will never allow
a conversation to grow, for he hates every kind of
natural growth. He has his own idea of what the
universe ought to be, and he tries to twist everything
into conformity with it. Great men, of course, may
have a passion for reforming the world, but they
would reform it in great matters. The prig begins
and usually ends with trifles. He judges men by
little things, and puts them against him from the
start by correcting them on points of no importance.
They resent his airs of superiority because they feel

that he sets himself very easy tasks. For him life is a game with simple and trivial rules which he has made for himself, and he expects everyone else to keep them. Because these rules satisfy him he is quite unaware of the complexity of reality. He does not know that it takes all sorts to make a world, and he is coldly hostile to everyone who is not of his own kind.

There are moral, intellectual, and æsthetic prigs; and nowadays the æsthetic prig is the commonest. The moral prig flourished most among the Puritans, and he was still common through a great part of the nineteenth century. He used to call himself and his friends serious people, and condemned every one who was not serious in little things. There has been a violent reaction against him, and now the immoral prig is more common than the moral. He is not usually immoral in practice, but he would like to be thought so. He uses the word " serious " as a term of abuse, but is himself desperately serious in his contempt of the Ten Commandments, though he talks against them more than he acts. His case is peculiarly unhappy, for he spends his life in trying to prove that he is not a prig and in proving that he is one. Prigs alone are filled with a morbid fear of priggishness.

The intellectual prig has never been very common in England, for he arouses little interest or resentment. More women, perhaps, than men are intellectual prigs; and their foible is often extreme accuracy in trifles. They are at the mercy of intellectual fashions, and they get their fashions from Germany.

They will condemn a great scholar, when he is old, because of a misprint which some one else has found in one of his books. They are also wonderfully quick in adopting new theories, and will think meanly of anyone who betrays ignorance of a theory which they had never heard of a week ago. In this they resemble the æsthetic prig, who is far more common and conspicuous. For him taste is a religion, and a very dogmatic one. But the articles of his creed, and indeed his very divinities, are always changing. His chief desire is to keep ahead of other prigs ; to worship the oldest Italian primitive or the newest French symbolist ; and nothing pleases him so much as to find another prig still worshipping the primitive of last year or not aware that the impressionists are no longer to be worshipped. He is as much concerned about his own salvation as the religious prig of the past, and he is equally sure that very few will be saved besides himself. He regards the great mass of mankind as æsthetically lost, and will have no dealings with them. He judges people inexorably by the aspect of their drawing-rooms. If these are middle Victorian, he takes no further interest in them. Thus he lives in a little world of his own just as much as any spinster in a country town.

This is the main evil of all priggishness, that it cuts the prig off from reality and experience. One of the chief difficulties of life is to have fixed principles and yet to learn from experience. The prig is like an artist whose principles are so fixed that they prevent him from looking at the visible world. It is hard to grow and at the same time to grow in the right way, and therefore the prig refuses to grow at all. He regards himself as ready-made, and is only careful that life shall not spoil him. He looks to experience only for proofs that he is right; and where he does not find them, he disregards it. Life is not an adventure to him, because he never expects it to change him. He has come into the world to teach, not to learn; and, like a bad schoolmaster, he learns nothing from his pupils.

Thus he deteriorates all through his life; for in spite of himself he is alive and cannot refuse to change with years. But since he will not grow, his changes are all for the worse. The complete prig is troublesome in youth, but intolerable in old age; and luckily he is very rare. Many men who are absurd prigs at twenty have lost all their priggishness at thirty; indeed, it is not a good sign for a youth to have no priggishness. It means that he is likely to grow too compliant to the world, since he will do nothing to offend it when he is young. For the priggishness of youth comes from the natural desire of a new generation not to be exactly like the last one, from the wish to start afresh and remake the world into something better than the middle-aged have made it. Youth is apt to suppose that the middle-aged are entirely satisfied with the world because they do not complain much about it; the fact being that they are merely used to its imperfections. Youth is not used to them, and sees no reason why they should not be mended at a stroke; at any rate, it will make war upon those imperfections which irk it most. Thus it often attacks imperfections which are mere symptoms of a deeper evil, and in doing so falls into priggishness. But this kind of priggishness wears off only too quickly. It is a mere newness, like the over-bright colours of a picture just painted. And as a picture that is over-bright will bear time better than one that is artificially mellow, so a young prig is likely to make a better man than a youth who is quite content with the world as he finds it.

THE COWARDICE OF YOUTH

YOUTH is admitted to be careless and cruel, but indulgence is claimed for these failings on the strength of courage. We see youth as gay and dashing; we imagine it in bright armour, forcing its way through thickets where knowledge and patience lie tangled, conquering with its virgin sword giants and blatant beasts whom experience is afraid to attack. *Si jeunesse savait, si vieillesse pouvait!* we sigh; and all the while we envy in our secret hearts the ignorance of youth, which we persuade ourselves to be merely a blessed ignorance of danger.

Youth is not afraid, we say; youth does not know what the dangers are, and the dangers melt away before its splendid ignorance. Safe conventions, the public order, accommodation and adjustment—of these youth knows nothing. It is sufficient for itself, and needs no bolstering with the down or sheltering with the screens which we of middle age, bruised and wary after our encounters with life, have constructed for our comfort. If we have any faith in man, we enjoy, with a kind of submissive fondness, the din made by " the younger generation knocking at the door." It is going to bundle us out of our comfortable habitation ; but then how fine a place it is going to make of it ! Youth will clear away our dusty, musty furniture, and throw the windows wide and flood the old house with air and light ! Youth will blunder, of course, but its blunders will be noble blunders ; youth is insensitive and hard ; but we are glad to pay that price for its high confidence, its gay courage.

Such is the common view. It has the authority of tradition, and no one begins to doubt its truth until he begins to look straight at the youth of his acquaint- ance. Then he will be fortunate if he does not meet with cases in which it appears romantic, and (unlike most romance) the flat opposite of the truth. A schoolboy or an undergraduate has his intellectual and emotional confidence. Under the shadow of medieval walls, under the care of medieval institutions, he will hold, or at least pronounce—and sometimes for so long as a month on end—opinions so " advanced " as to amuse his teachers and frighten his parents. There is nothing to prevent his doing so, and no courage is needed to make a brave show of independence. Take the same hothead after he has been for a year or two in the world, and it too often happens that you will find no trace of- the courage of youth. Too often it

Modern Essays

is the young men who cling for safety to the accepted opinion and the comfort of public order; the young men who dread the exceptional in circumstance and character, who sneer at experiment, and would see the world " run " according to the norm of the bricklayer, which is the slowest work of the slowest worker. And no doubt there is every excuse for them. Impatient of restraint, and contemptuous of educational tradition, they flung out into a world that was to make easy way for them; and after one tussle they found themselves scuttling for protection to the rear of the slow-moving main army. And there, unable to boast of courage, they will boast of their prudence and appeal to the wisdom of numbers.

It must not be supposed that their case is hopeless. Theirs will never be the greatness of the few who are brave from birth till death, and, as life goes on, add to courage and gaiety the sympathy and understanding of experience. But they will, if they are not terrified out of spiritual existence, some day be middle-aged; and in the middle-aged men who have kept their faith lie the courage and purpose of the world. The middle-aged man knows what youth can never know—what it is that he wants for himself and for society. He knows his own strength and his own weakness, which he has learned whether he would or not. Amid moral and social man's array of adjustments and accommodations with reality, amid his means of protection against the truth, he has made up his mind which are worth preserving and which are not. And, unless he has the misfortune to be among those who are born sneerers, the middle-aged man, finding his enthusiasm grow with his experience, can afford a pitying smile for youth's general claim to courage.

CHARLATANS

EVERYONE affects to despise charlatans; yet in real life a splendid charlatan often gives great pleasure even to those who see through him. He never disappoints, for it is his business not to disappoint. His imitation of genius, like so many other imitations, is far more effective than the reality. The aim of the real genius is to do his work, whatever it may be; success to him is only a by-product, pleasant enough, perhaps, but not necessary; and very likely he does not know how to enjoy it when he gets it. The author of a masterpiece is led into a crowd of his admirers, who expect to see him with the glory of inspiration round his brows; and he comes blinking and distraught, a workman dragged from his workshop, thinking not of what he has done, but of what he wants to do. All his energy is spent in being a genius; and he has none to spare for behaving like one. But the charlatan's business is to behave like one; he gives all his energy up to that, and he does it far better than the genius himself. If he is a charlatan writer, even in the act of composition he is behaving like a genius, and doing it so well that he deceives himself before he deceives the world. Indeed, the

successful charlatan must deceive himself. A genius
like Molière may test his work to some extent upon
his housekeeper. From her he will learn, not whether
it is altogether good or bad, but whether a certain
effect will tell upon all the world. But the charlatan
must be his own " foolometer," since he works only
for effect. In the very moment of composition he is
audience as well as author. He writes every sentence
for his own answering applause ; and, if he gets it,
hopes for the applause of the world. Unless he had
himself for gallery, he would never play at all ; for to
him the work itself is nothing—its effect everything.
He must be thrilled by his own tricks before he can
have the heart to play them.

But his true life begins when he comes before the
world ; his true art consists, not in producing sham
works of genius, but in behaving as if they were real.
And he has a genuine imaginative delight in this
business, which communicates itself to an unenvious
spectator. He is like a stage king, always crowned
and sceptred, and how much more regal than a real
king busy with the affairs of his kingdom ! When
Garrick and Barry were playing King Lear at the same
time in London, an epigram was written upon their
performances, of which the last two lines run thus :

" A King—aye every inch a king, such Barry doth appear.
   But Garrick's quite another thing—he's every inch King
      Lear."

Such in real life is the difference between the man of
genius and the charlatan. The charlatan appears

every inch a man of genius ; but Michelangelo or
Mozart is just himself. And as those who went to
the play to see a king behaving as such no doubt
preferred Barry to Garrick, so those who want to see
a man of genius behaving as such will prefer the charlatan to the divine artist. They look for an effect,
and the charlatan produces it ; he conforms to their
idea of what he ought to be, and they reward him
with their applause. In this applause he takes so
much delight that it is a pleasure to watch him. He
is not sordid. It is praise he wants more than pudding ;
" the roaring and the wreaths " rather than the
cheque which they imply.

It is commonly supposed that the man who gets the
palm without the dust will not enjoy it. But the
charlatan spends his life in enjoying the palm just
because he has not earned it. The true man of genius
is used to his genius, as the true king is used to his
kingship ; but the charlatan never grows used to his
pretence of genius, and never tires of persuading himself and the world that it is a reality.

If there is indeed no more reality in life and no more
significance than he finds in it, then all is well with
him, and it is as good to be a charlatan as a man of
genius. But if otherwise—well, then, perhaps there
is truth in that fate with which the button-moulder
threatens Peer Gynt. For he is a charlatan so complete that he loses his own identity altogether in the
different parts that he plays ; and at the end there
is nothing of him left to damn. At any rate that is
a true story of the works of the charlatan ; they

indeed are quickly lost " in the infinite azure of the past," for they never have had an independent existence, and never have expressed anything except their author's pretence that he is what he is not. From the first they belong to an unreal world of effect— that is to say, of effect without cause.

For when we say of a charlatan that he does everything for effect, we mean that he tries to produce effects without causes, as, for instance, the effect of genius without genius itself. And he is subject to this condition—that he must produce these causeless effects upon himself before he can produce them on others. So the complete and triumphant charlatan, who is always producing causeless effects upon himself, loses all sense of cause and effect and comes to live in a world that has no reality, a world where two and two make any number he wishes them to make. To some extent he infects everyone who believes in him with this unreality; but not fatally, for they can recover when his influence is withdrawn. But he himself is always subject to his own unreality. It is the cause of his success, and success increases it. If some great disaster befalls him, it may show him what he is, and so bring him salvation; but if not, if he prospers always, then indeed he gains the whole world at the price of his own soul more certainly than the most cynical villain.

Modern Essays

ON FRIENDSHIP

FRIENDSHIP is above reason, for, though you find virtues in a friend, he was your friend before you found them. It is a gift that we offer because we must ; to give it as the reward of virtue would be to set a price upon it, and those who do that have no friendship to give. If you choose your friends on the ground that you are virtuous and want virtuous company, you are no nearer to true friendship than if you choose them for commercial reasons. Besides, who are you that you should be setting a price upon your friendship ? It is enough for any man that he has the divine power of making friends, and he must leave it to that power to determine who his friends shall be. For, though you may choose the virtuous to be your friends, they may not choose you ; indeed, friendship cannot grow where there is any calculated choice. It comes, like sleep, when you are not thinking about it ; and you should be grateful, without any misgiving, when it comes.

So no man who knows what friendship is ever gave up a friend because he turns out to be disreputable. His only reason for giving up a friend is that he has ceased to care for him ; and, when that happens, he should reproach himself for this mortal poverty of affection, not the friend for having proved unworthy. For it is inhuman presumption to say of any man that he is unworthy of your friendship, just as it is

24

to say of any woman, when you have fallen out of love with her, that she is unworthy of your love. In friendship and in love we are always humble, because we see that a free gift has been given to us; and to lose that humility because we have lost friendship or love is to take a pride in what should shame us.

We have our judgments and our penalties as part of the political mechanism that is forced upon us so that we may continue to live; but friendship is not friendship at all unless it teaches us that these are not part of our real life. They have to be; and we pay men, and clothe them in wigs and scarlet, to sit in judgment on other men. So we are tempted to play this game of judgment ourselves, even though no one has paid us to do it. It is only in the warmth of friendship that we see how cold a thing it is to judge and how stupid to take a pleasure in judging; for we recognise this warmth as a positive good, a richness in our natures, while the coldness that sets us judging is a poverty. Just as our criticism of a work of art begins only when we have ceased to experience it, so our criticism of our friends begins only when we have ceased to experience them, when our minds can no longer remain at the height of intimacy. But this criticism is harmless if we know it for what it is, merely the natural reaction, the cold fit that comes after the warm, and if we do not suppose that our coldness is wiser than our warmth.

There are men who cannot be friends except when they are under an illusion that their friends are perfect, and when the illusion passes there is an end of their friendship. But true friendship has no illusions, for it reaches to that part of a man's nature that is beyond his imperfections, and in doing so it takes all of them for granted. It does not even assume that he is better than other men, for there is egotism in assuming that. A man is your friend, not because of his superiorities, but because there is something open from your nature to his, a way that is closed between you and most men. You and he understand each other, as the phrase is ; your relation with him is a rare success among a multitude of failures, and if you are proud of the success you should be ashamed of the failure.

There is nothing so fatal to friendship as this egotism of accounting for it by some superiority in the friend. If you do that you will become a member of a set, all, in their assertion of each other's merits, implying their own, and all uneasy lest they are giving more than they get. For if you insist upon the virtues of your friend, you expect him to insist upon your virtues, and there is a competition between you which makes friendship a burden rather than a rest. Criticism then becomes a treachery, for it implies that you are beginning to doubt those superiorities upon which your friendship is supposed to be based. But when no superiorities are assumed, criticism is only the exercise of a natural curiosity. It is because a man is your friend, and you like him so much and know him so well, that you are curious about him. You are in fact an expert upon him, and like to show your expert knowledge. And you are an expert because

in the warmth of friendship his disguises melt away
from him, and he shows himself to you just as he is.
Indeed, that is the test of friendship and the delight
of it, that because we are no longer afraid of being
thought worse than we are we do not try to seem
better. We know that it is not our virtues that have
won us friendship, and we do not fear to lose it through
our vices. We have reached that blessed state of
being nearer to heaven than anything else in this
life, in which affection does not depend upon judgment ; and we are like gods, who have no need even
to forgive, because they know. It is a rare state, and
never attained to in its perfection. We can approach
it only if we know what friendship is and really desire
it, and especially if we admire the man who is a friend
without ever wondering at his choice of friends or
blaming him for his faithfulness to them whatever
evil they may do.

ON UNDERSTANDING OTHERS

AT intervals something happens which brings it
forcibly home to us that we are lacking in the power
of understanding or imagining other people's feelings
and of putting ourselves, in however slight a degree,
in their places. Such an event is a criminal trial in
a foreign court. Even those who have not by failing
in a legal career earned a prescriptive right to consider
themselves persons of clear and logical mind stand

utterly dumbfounded. It is not only that every
Briton has been so well brought up on the maxim
that "What the soldier said is not evidence" that
he has been alternately puzzled and irritated by the
apparent irrelevance of nearly all the topics introduced
into the case; he has found himself wondering over
and over again why certain remarks should appear
to him of no great import and yet should put the
whole court and the whole populace outside the court
in a frenzy; he has had to admit that there are more
things that he is incapable even of beginning to understand than he had hitherto deemed possible. If he is
not by nature so arrogant that this lack of understanding only swells his arrogance, and he puts all
such incomprehensible matters and sentiments on one
side with Mr. Podsnap's comment of "Not English,"
he should feel himself now at the end of the trial to
be a more humble-minded person and one of larger
sympathies than he did at the beginning.

The power of entering into other people's feelings is
one that grows on us with age, so that any satisfaction we may derive from the consciousness of a gentler
and more understanding judgment of our fellows is
counterbalanced by the knowledge that the years
have begun their deadly work in earnest. The very
young are rarely very sympathetic or considerate.
They do not credit others with any of the little sensi-
tivenesses of which they are themselves conscious,
and so touch them unwittingly on the raw in a manner
which would be called brutal and callous in their
elders. When they chance to find out that another

has thought, or felt, or suffered something common to the whole human race, the discovery gives them a shock of genuine surprise.

On the other hand, this should fairly be said for them : that if they do not believe that others can be as sensitive as they are, so also they do not credit them with all their own vanities and meannesses and trumpery manœuvrings. These things they know to be contemptible in their own case, but they fancy the shame of them to be theirs alone ; they cannot imagine the more disgraceful of such weaknesses to exist even in the breasts of those whom they dislike or deride—and the number of those whom we dislike is in youth usually a large one.

When we grow older we come to walk more carefully and not to tread so cruelly upon the toes of our fellows. We have had our own toes more often lacerated, and we have come dimly to see that other people are much as we are. Even if we cannot picture them clearly to ourselves as feeling in quite the same way as we do, we come to appreciate by a kind of rule of thumb the overwhelming probability that they in fact do so. The things that make us hot and uncomfortable appear ridiculously trifling in the case of others, but we can make allowances. More than that, to be quite just to ourselves, we are not merely actuated by motives of expediency : we do really entertain kindlier and more sympathetic sentiments towards them. We used actually to hate people ; now we only find them tiresome; and this change of feeling makes us the more generally indulgent.

29

Modern Essays

So far increasing age may be said to bring with it only clear gain, but there is another side to the picture. Because we understand better than we did that our neighbours are of the same stuff as we are, we often see through them with a fatal clarity of vision. At school we did not know how much we hurt them by disparaging remarks as to their parents or their personal appearance, but neither could we believe what wretched, underhand things they would do, or at any rate would like to have done, in order to gain some advantage for themselves or to spite some one of whom they were jealous. Now, judging them by our own shortcomings, we can believe these things of them, and, granted that power of believing, we can read them sometimes like a printed book.

On the whole, setting the advantages and disadvantages fairly against one another, the balance is in favour of age, and we grow more generally charitable as we grow older. Thus we live more at peace with our neighbours, which is a pleasant thing to do, and they become the more interesting to us in that we can make a better guess at what is going on in their minds. It may be that we are sometimes over-indulgent and miss something of real value, in the downright condemnations of youth, but the danger of being over-charitable is a comparatively remote one. And it is a consolation, though perhaps not a very worthy one, that we may fairly hope that others, in the same stage of senile decay, will not think too bitterly and ungenerously of us.

Modern Essays

COLLECTORS

THE collector's instinct sems to be a curious by-product of the human mind; and not only of the human mind, for magpies, monkeys, and even dogs sometimes have it. When a dog makes a store of bones, old and entirely fleshless, he is like the collector who keeps obsolete things just because they are obsolete. A used postage stamp is to a man very much what a bone without flesh is to a dog; but the collector of postage stamps goes further than the dog, in that he prefers an old postage stamp to a new one, while no dog, however ardent a collector of bones without flesh, would not rather have a bone with flesh on it. Yet there is more method in the human collector, since he has always before him the ideal of a complete collection, whereas no dog, probably, ever dreamed of acquiring specimens of all the different kinds of bones there are in the world.

This ideal of a complete collection is the usual spur of the human collector; and often he will collect the most out-of-the-way things in the hope of attaining it. But there is also the spur of rivalry; and because of that there are not many collectors of things that no one else collects. Every collector likes to have at least one rival, whom he may outdo and from whom, perhaps, he may steal; for the collector's instinct is sometimes too strong for the most honest of men, so that they come to regard stealing as only a bold and skilful kind of collecting. They would never steal anything except what they collect; but in stealing a fine specimen they are only rectifying the iniquity of chance which has given that specimen to an ignoramus who does not deserve it. For them collecting is a game, and stealing is not a breach of the rules. Indeed, there is only one breach of the rules—namely, forging. But even forgeries make collecting more exciting; and perhaps they are not really a breach of the rules, but only an added complication in the game, a new kind of bunker, so to speak, which tests the skill of the player.

We may take it that the most perfect example of the collector is one who collects articles neither useful nor beautiful in themselves with the sole purpose of attaining to a complete collection. For him collecting is altogether a game, and it has the peculiar merit of a game in that it gives him an object which he can entirely accomplish. In real life we cannot entirely accomplish anything. Even Alexander could not conquer the whole world. Even Michelangelo can never have expressed all that he wanted to express in his art. Indeed, the more full of life a man is, the more he tries to do greater things than he can do. In games we escape from the infinities of reality. We propose for ourselves a finite and absolute end; and if we win we accomplish this and for the moment taste the delight of an imaginary Heaven. It is the desire to escape from the inconclusiveness of reality that sets us playing games. In life we never know whether we have lost or won, but in games we do know, when the game is over; and so there are some who can give more passion to games than to business, because in the one case the end is clear and finite, in the other it is not.

Now the collector is one who makes a game of the business of acquiring property. The man who sets to work to acquire property at large has no aim which he can utterly accomplish. He cannot acquire all the property in the world; and there is no one to tell him when he has enough. But the collector makes arbitrary rules about the property which he sets out to acquire. He will collect what most people do not want, and he will be content with specimens of all the varieties of what he collects. The more rules he makes, the more likely he is to accomplish his aim. But if he makes too many rules his game will be too easy. Most collectors play a game which takes them all their lives, and which they do not win at the end. But even so, it is a game much simpler than life itself, and one in which there is a series of unmistakable triumphs. Each new specimen means a step nearer to the goal; but there are not many men who feel that they are always advancing nearer to the goal of existence—not many, indeed, who have a clear idea of the nature of that goal. So they like to set up arbitrary goals for themselves and to feel all the glory of victory in a contest, unreal indeed, but difficult enough to seem real.

Many collectors, of course, do not make a complete game of collecting. The miser, for instance, collects money; but he knows that he can never collect even a small part of all the money in the world. He is unwise, because he plays a game with all the defects of unreality but with none of its consolations. He cannot win ; and yet he is not doing what is worth doing for its own sake.

Again, the man who collects works of art is not playing a complete game. He collects objects that are valuable and much prized for themselves ; and very likely he himself prizes them, not merely because he has chosen to collect them, but because they are beautiful. Also he can never hope to make a complete collection. Yet he is a collector as soon as he buys objects not only because he likes them, but as specimens ; as soon as he begins to hoard them and ceases to employ them for use and ornament.

There is some misunderstanding of the function of art in all collectors of works of art ; for in collections works of art are estranged from their proper environment and use. Just as money is not performing its function when hoarded in a safe, so works of art are not performing their function when hoarded in a collection. China loses its significance in a china cabinet ; and even pictures, if they are good, lose part of their significance in a picture gallery. And the worst of it is that works of art come to be produced for collectors ; that china is made to put in cabinets, and pictures are painted to hang in galleries. Such things may be pretty enough, but in them art is turning into the pieces of a game and losing its necessary and vital connection with reality. We do art an injury when we play a game with it ; for it is a part of life, and

should be treated quite seriously, like life itself. It is
well to treasure works of art for their beauty, and
better still to use them and enjoy their use. But it
is not well to collect them for the mere pleasure of
collecting, as if they were postage stamps. It is this
kind of collecting that gives a huge and arbitrary
value to works of certain periods and makes people
prize them not for their beauty but for their style.
Those who have an itch for the game of collecting had
better collect postage stamps than pictures, for they
do no indignity to postage stamps when they treat
them as mere counters in a game; but pictures, if
they are worth anything, deserve to be treasured for
themselves.

ON GIVING ADVICE

BEFORE you give advice, that is to say advice which
you have not been asked to give, it is well to put to
yourself two questions—namely, what is your motive
for giving it, and what is it likely to be worth? If
these questions were always asked, and honestly answered, there would be less advice given. People who
want to give advice always assume that they do so
from the highest motives. It is to save the other
party from some manifest error or sin; and it is because of their affection or regard for the other party
that they feel this desire to save. They assume this;
but it is never safe to assume that your own motives
are lofty, for the very assumption is usually a sign

that they are not. Our motives are loftiest when we are not conscious of their loftiness, and particularly when we are not enjoying our own sense of it. But, as a matter of fact, if we feel a strong desire to give advice to anyone, we do not usually feel at the same time a strong affection or regard for them. The desire to give advice is itself a symptom of disapproval; and further, it is usually the result of a desire to express that disapproval. And we are most moved to give advice to those for whom our affection and regard may be taken for granted, but to whom we would rather express our disapproval. We cannot go to them and say that we disapprove of them. That would not be affectionate, and might lead to reprisals. But we can give them advice in which the disapproval is implied and which yet seems innocently helpful.

And it is just because disapproval is implied but not openly expressed in advice that it is resented. If a man comes to you and tells you that he disapproves of you, you can reply that you disapprove of him; and there is an end of it. But if he comes offering you advice, he professes to do it out of pure friendliness, and that is what you do not believe and yet cannot disapprove.

Advice, of course, implies criticism, and raises at once the question what right the adviser has to criticise, which is the second that he should ask himself. Is he wiser than the man whom he wishes to advise; or has he any special knowledge of the subject on which he feels that his advice is needed ? If it is merely a question of his superior wisdom, he may

take it for granted that his own opinion on that point
will not be shared by the other party ; and also that
we are apt to be most unwise when we believe most
firmly in our own wisdom, indeed that the itch to give
advice is itself a sign that we are not at our wisest.
But, even if we are sure of our own special knowledge,
it may be that the other party has consulted another
expert, whose knowledge seems to him greater than
ours ; and on that point we shall no more be able
to convince him than on the point of our general
superiority in wisdom. However tactful we may be in
our manner of offering advice, he will still see the intention to criticise behind it, and will still wonder angrily
why we have more right to criticise him than he to
criticise us. And that is a question which we usually
cannot answer ; at least if we tried to answer it, we
should have told so many home truths that we should
probably hear a good many in return ; and the final
result would be a quarrel.

All these things are well known to people who know
themselves, and they therefore are usually careful not
to give advice until it is asked for. The people who
are most lavish of advice are those who do not know
themselves, and who are, therefore, always able to
find the loftiest motives for what they most want to
do. It is delicious to feel your own superiority to
anyone else, and still more delicious to imply it without openly stating it. But pleasures of the kind are
costly, for they destroy friendships that are worth
more than any egotistical pleasure. Therefore the
best rule for those who wish to give advice is that they

shall not give it if they feel any pleasure in doing so, for they may be sure that the pleasure is not a healthy one.

There are people who cannot enjoy a pleasure unless they have first persuaded themselves that it is a duty. They are perhaps the most confirmed hedonists of all, for they are not content to enjoy without the added delight of conscious rectitude. But it is just this added delight which the rest of mankind grudge them; and that probably is the real reason why we resent advice which we have not asked for. We feel that the man who gives it is enjoying his own sense of duty, and at our expense. If he wants the animal pleasure of telling us what he thinks of us, we would rather that he indulged himself in it frankly, for then he would give us an opportunity for the same frank indulgence. We should both, at least, be on equal terms; but when he comes with his sense of duty, we are not prepared with a like sense of duty against him, or with advice to give in return for his. And yet those who are readiest to give advice are usually those who seem to need it most, and perhaps the best way to counter them is to give them advice about giving advice.

CURIOSITY

An action once heard in the Law Courts turned on the question of a letter, in an open envelope and bearing a halfpenny stamp, which was read by a servant.

Modern Essays

The servant, on being pressed as to his reasons for reading it, ultimately made the very natural admission that he was curious; and it is probable that a number of respectable and honourable people felt a measure of sympathy with him. There can scarcely be a duller mass of literature in the world than that which is written upon post-cards. Nevertheless, there are few who do not feel a desire to read some one else's post-card, and, if the card chance to lie face upwards on the table, there may even be few who do not yield to the desire. There is a childish delight in finding something out for ourselves that is almost universally felt; the more interesting the discovery the better, but the great thing is to make a discovery of some sort.

Everybody who was properly brought up—that is to say, who was brought up on Hans Andersen—remembers the story of the Swineherd. The King's son had his addresses and also his beautiful presents rejected by the proud Emperor's daughter. Having disguised himself, he obtained the post of swineherd to the Emperor, and while following that occupation he invented a kettle possessing this magical property, that anyone putting his finger in the steam could at once discover by the smell what every family in the town was having for dinner. The Princess, who had rejected the most fragrant of roses and the most melodious of nightingales offered by a royal suitor, was so enthralled by the kettle that she consented to buy it from the lowly swineherd at the price of ten kisses; and then she and her ladies in waiting spent a whole day in discovering that the Lord Chamberlain was eating pancakes and the shoemaker sour krout.

This Princess was by no means unique, for there are to-day many ladies living in small towns who without the aid of any magic kettle aspire to attain to an almost uncanny knowledge. If their neighbours were voluntarily to inform them every day what they were going to have for dinner, the knowledge would even at first give but little pleasure, and would soon become an intolerable nuisance. It is the feeling of being an adventurer upon hidden seas of knowledge that makes all the difference, and those of us who do not happen to be interested in legs of mutton can probably find parallel and convincing instances in our own case. Any despot who should desire a punishment to fit the crime of curiosity would not have far to seek. He would merely marshal all the friends and relations of the criminal, and bid them pour into the wretch's ears the fullest details of their own affairs.

There are, no doubt, just a few people to whom this would be no punishment at all. They have a power of taking a genuine, lasting, and sympathetic interest in the concerns of others, and their qualities must be written very plainly on their faces, for everybody confides in them. Not only do their own friends come to them for sympathy, but there is something about their demeanour which Mr. Yellowplush would have called "beneviolent," compelling total strangers to open their hearts; they have to read love letters in public places, even as Mr. Pickwick had to listen to the hopes of Mr. Peter Magnus at the Great White

Horse in Ipswich, though as a rule without such disastrous and far-reaching consequences.

These rare creatures, however, cannot fairly be called curious; the interest they take in the business of others is altogether too kindly a one for that. It has to be admitted that with most of us there is in the desire to find out about our friends an element of unkindness. If our discoveries do not give us a small thrill of self-righteousness or of malevolent amusement, we feel just a little flat and disappointed. The Princess and her ladies did not merely want to know what the neighbours were having for dinner. They wanted to be able to titter together over the meanness of the Lord Chamberlain in having no smarter dish on his table than pancakes, or to hold up their hands in horror at the extravagance of the shoemaker for having even as much as sour krout. If we were all entirely kind-hearted and charitable, there would perhaps be no need even to attempt to resist the temptation of reading our friends' post-cards.

UGLINESS

SIGNOR BENEDETTO CROCE, the great æsthetic philosopher, says that ugliness is always the result of failure of expression. That is a theory which allures us because of its orderly and rational simplicity, but it does not seem to cover all kinds of ugliness, even of things made by man. Take, for instance, the case of motor-horns or hooters, which are again rousing something like a general popular revolt. The sounds they make are hideous ; but one cannot say that they are inexpressive. On the contrary, they express, very clearly, a strong desire on the part of those who use them to clear everyone and everything out of the way at all costs. And we dislike them as much as we dislike the desire itself, just because they are so expressive of the desire. They are like those bad manners which are not merely failure or gaucherie, but a clear expression, or betrayal, of a disagreeable character.

Iago, for instance, is ugly in his manners, or would be ugly if we could encounter him in real life ; but he is not, and never could be, inexpressive. Yet the ugliness of his manners would not be intentional ugliness ; it would be betrayal, not designed expression, and the result of a discord rather than a harmony. And so it is with everything that is brutally and aggressively ugly in our modern life. All these things do express something, but something which no one would like to express about himself. They tell secrets, and they are ugly because the secrets are ugly. The hooter, for instance, tells us ugly secrets about our relations with each other. It is typical of a state of mind which religion and civilisation have failed to destroy ; of an egotism which merely uses civilisation for its own purposes, and is the more brutal because it is powerful by means of civilised appliances.

That is the peculiar grossness of the ugliness of our time. Brute instincts in a brute are what we expect ;

42

and there is no incongruity in them. If a tiger snarls over his food, he is merely expressing an instinct with the means that nature has given to him. But in our ugliness we are often expressing brute instincts with the means that civilisation has given us for a better purpose; and it is the incongruity between the means and the end that produces the ugliness. There is great ingenuity in the hooter, but it has all been used to make a brutally animal noise, the kind of noise that an elephant might make if he wished to clear smaller animals out of his way when he was going down to the river to drink. He uses only his own physical power, but the "scorching" motorist is using an intellectual power, not his own, as if he were an elephant.

So Iago used all the subtleties of civilisation to gratify an instinct in its essence purely bestial; for he wanted something which he had not got, and all the spiritual part of his mind lowered itself to gratify his rage that he could not get it. So he was uglier than any angry beast could be, with the ugliness of perversion and of incongruity between the end and the means used for it. He was like an artist who prostitutes a skill given by the spirit for some fleshly purpose; and there is this prostitution in all the ugliness peculiar to civilisation and in the bad manners of civilised brutes. They use the faculties of their own minds, and those which they have inherited from other minds, for purposes merely animal. To them all the gifts of disinterested science or thought are only weapons in the struggle for life. They are armoured like the rhinoceros, but with armour that never could have existed if mankind had been what they will to be. They are powerful with a stolen power which they would use to destroy all the higher instincts that have produced it.

That incongruity between higher means and a lower end is the essence of this ugliness, which we must distinguish from the ugliness of mere failure. The artist who tries to express something noble and fails produces a work which displeases us with its inadequacy. He seems to tell us what he has attempted, and then to disappoint us by not doing it. But in this other kind of ugliness there is no conscious effort at the expression of anything high or low, but merely the betrayal of an unpleasant state of mind. Here, if there is failure at all, it is failure to keep an ugly secret, which we cannot call failure of expression. But the secret is ugly just because it is incongruous with the means by which it expresses itself. It would not be ugly, or a secret, in a brute. It is both in a man, because all the achievements of men are based upon an assumption that men are not brutes; and, when a man uses these achievements for a brutal end, he betrays a discord from which the brutes are free.

Signor Croce might say, perhaps, that it is the discord of conflict, and that conflict means failure of expression; but it seems to be rather the discord of a base victory that can bring no peace. For it means that the brute has conquered the man, and is using human qualities for its own purpose. We expect, whatever our theories of life may be, to see the lower

44

instincts used in the service of the higher; and when
we see the higher used in the service of the lower we
are shocked, as if at an indecency. The discord there
is a discord not between different parts of the same
nature, but between that nature and our idea of the
universe. The ugliness, in fact, is positive, not merely
negative. It is the ugliness of perversion rather than
of failure, of something that must be destroyed if it
is not to destroy all that we most value.

MORAL INDIGNATION

It is a curious fact that many people who think they
have cured themselves of the love of pleasure, and
who at any rate refuse to take a natural pleasure in
pleasant things, do yet enjoy the exercise of their
moral sense as much as the greedy enjoy eating. They
may not be conscious of their enjoyment, but that
only makes it the more exquisite to them. They are
epicures who want a pleasure free from the obvious
sweetness of vulgar pleasures, a savoury with a sharp
or bitter taste for the mind, and one, too, which they
can persuade themselves has a medicinal quality;
and they find it in moral indignation. For that begins
with pain, but with a pain that does not really hurt,
since it is caused by the evil-doing of others; and it
passes quickly into a pleasure, which is all the greater
because it began as a pain. It is in fact of the same
nature as the fierce animal pleasure caused by scratch-

ing an irritable place ; and those who have once learned to enjoy their moral indignation soon learn also to cultivate in themselves a moral irritability which is constantly demanding the relief they instantly give it. The world is for them a vale of tears ; but they manage to weep very comfortably in it, because they are always weeping for other people, and because their tears are angry. For no one is really sad so long as he is angry, since there is always some mixture of pleasure in anger, or at least in the expression of it ; and these people think it a duty to express their anger as soon as they feel it. In fact, they have learned better than anyone else how to combine duty with pleasure ; and yet we all dislike them, even if they persuade us to respect them.

We prefer the frank pleasure-lover, for he at least does enjoy what is meant to be enjoyed ; but morality is not meant to be enjoyed so long as it remains morality. It is, and it ought to be, a disagreeable necessity ; for it means doing things, not by instinct, but by compulsion. It implies, in fact, a conflict of the mind, and only when that conflict is over can the mind be at rest. Its aim is to produce a habit of well-doing and well-being, and the man who has acquired that habit can enjoy it as an artist enjoys his art. But if anyone had ever completely acquired that habit there would be an end of morals for him, and he would be a natural man again with a perfect nature.

Unfortunately, we none of us have attained to this state ; and, when we enjoy our moral indignation, we are perverting morality from its proper function. This we do by the simple means of allowing our moral sense to concern itself with others rather than with ourselves. By a curious twist of the mind we succeed in feeling about other people what we ought to be feeling about ourselves. In fact, we make them our moral whipping-boys; and when we have suffered an unreal and vicarious concern for their sins we have all the relief that ought to come only of penitence for our own. It is always painful to compare yourself with what you ought to be; and if you can satisfy your moral sense by comparing other people with what they ought to be, you escape this pain, and indeed substitute a very subtle pleasure for it. You become a kind of public accountant, instead of a private one who is forced to face the discrepancy between his own assets and liabilities. Other people may not like you for your ruthless presentment of their balance-sheets, but, since you never look at your own, you continue to like yourself, and you succeed in doing that when, to everyone else, it seems to have become an impossible task.

The worst of moral indignation is that it never produces the effects confidently expected by the morally indignant. As the Chinese philosopher said, If you wish to convert a man you must persuade him that when he does well he is obeying the dictates of his own heart. He will not do well because you are angry with him for doing ill, since your anger seems to him a mere egotism that challenges his own. There is nothing like moral indignation for provoking a defence of the indefensible. Tell a man that he is wicked, and he will take sides with his own wickedness and arrest his own natural process of repentance. Since he feels you are unfair to him, he will put things right by being more than fair to himself.

And since moral indignation thus always fails of its supposed purpose, the morally indignant are always dissatisfied—not with themselves of course, but with the effects of their own virtue. They cannot enjoy their moral indignation quite simply, like an animal pleasure, for if they could do that it would cease to be moral indignation. They only get pleasure from it because they think it is a pain righteously endured ; and a real pain comes to them when no one gives them credit for their righteousness, and when it fails to produce the effect that righteousness ought to produce. The frank pleasure-lover at least has his fun, like the boy who eats his cake. But they try to eat their cake and have it, and, as we know, that can never be done in this life. Their desire is to refuse pleasure and yet to enjoy their refusal of it all at the same time. It is better to enjoy pleasure itself, for that at least is a positive, not a negative, enjoyment ; and it is possible to learn something from excess. But from the enjoyment of moral indignation we learn nothing except that our function in life is to judge other people, which it certainly is not.

Modern Essays

PARADOX

THE word paradox is commonly supposed to be a
term of abuse; but there is nothing abusive in its
meaning. It means what is contrary to the common
opinion, and that may be true or false. The value of
a paradoxical saying lies in its truth, not in its relation to what most people think. Yet most people
when they have called a saying a paradox think that
they have condemned it; as if every discovery in
thought were not a paradox, for if it were not a paradox it would not be a discovery. It is no abuse to
call an original writer a lover of paradox but a simple
statement of fact, for he does not want to discover
what everyone knows. The truths that he seeks and
delights to find are new and surprising ones, and the
surprise which they cause expresses itself in this word
paradox.

When Galileo discovered that the earth went round
the sun, that was a paradox, and one which the
Pope resented, as we all know. So every painter who
makes a discovery in his art paints a paradox. He
shows us what we have never seen before either in
pictures or in reality; and if we expect to see in
pictures nothing but what we have always seen in
them, we resent his discovery as the Pope resented
Galileo's. Why cannot he paint like the Old Masters?
we ask; and so we wonder why some new thinker
cannot think like the old ones. But the old thinkers,
if they were thinkers, did not think like the older

ones. If they had done that they would never have been remembered as thinkers. It was their paradoxes that established their authority ; and those paradoxes became common opinion when people were used to them. Mill, Adam Smith, Aristotle, and Plato, and, no doubt, Moses and Confucius, were all paradoxical in their time, and they have all been used as authorities against later discoverers.

A truth, when everybody believes it, is always abused, since it is believed for its convenience rather than its truth. It becomes a comfortable, established fact that blocks the way, instead of pointing it, to further inquiry. How angrily was the Darwinian theory opposed when it was new ; and, now that it is old, how lazily it is accepted by those who do not want to think any more about such things. They like it because it seems to them to explain everything ; but no theory, however true, does that. Indeed a truth is not a truth at all except to those who recognise it with a shock of discovery, who see in it something suddenly and wonderfully agreeable to their own experience. To the others it is merely a phrase which they repeat, as the Tibetan turns his prayer wheel, with a notion that they have done their duty by thought. But those repeated truths naturally disgust the discoverer ; and, being only human, he looks to see if he can find anything false in them. At any rate, he knows that they are no longer the truths which people heed ; they have become drugs rather than stimulants, and so he is tempted to put the case against them as strongly as he can.

Modern Essays

We can see this very clearly in contradictory proverbs, each of which was once, no doubt, a paradox and
became a platitude in its turn. The man who first
said " Look after the pence and the pounds will look
after themselves " was no doubt accused of uttering
a paradox; and indeed it was a paradox with a
dangerous element of truth in it. But it only became
really dangerous when it was a platitude flattering
to the petty caution of the mediocre; and then came
the corrective proverb, " Penny wise and pound
foolish; " and now both are platitudes which any fool
can use to justify his particular kind of folly.

It is often said that a thinker must be studied in
relation to his age, and this is supposed to mean that
what he thought all his contemporaries were thinking.
But usually his relation to his age consists in the fact
that he thought against it, and that not from mere
perversity but because all thought is partly opportunist. It deals with the problems of its own time,
and one of those is to correct the formulæ of its own
time. So, if we want to understand the excesses of a
thinker, we must take them to be provoked by contrary excesses. Plato insists upon the absolute because in his time there was a vicious insistence upon
the relative. Bacon makes too much of induction
because the contemporary vice of thought was to be
too deductive. Both were paradoxical, as, no doubt,
Jonah was paradoxical in Nineveh. There was a
great momentum of opinion against them, and they
had to exercise a counteracting energy which seems
irrational when the momentum no longer exists or

when they have transferred it to their own side.
Then the world accepts their opportunist paradoxes
for simple, absolute truth, and it becomes necessary
for a new thinker to be paradoxical against them. So
after Jeremy Bentham you have Ruskin, and after
the Romantics Mr. Shaw. There is truth in all of
them ; but the truth that is most wholesome for all
of us is the one which is unwelcome and surprising—
which is, in fact, a paradox. But if we accept a
paradox because it makes us feel clever to do so,
we are no wiser than those who accept a platitude
because it makes them feel comfortable. The proper
function of a paradox is to provoke thought, not self-
satisfaction. Indeed, if you accept it without thinking, you turn it into a platitude before its time.

RESPECTABILITY

Sarcasms against respectability are as common as
jokes about mothers-in-law, but the strange fact
about them is that they do not come from the disreputable. Most of these would enjoy the privileges
of respectability if they could, and submit to the
condemnation of the respectable without much com-
plaint. The theoretical rebels against respectability
are nearly all themselves respectable in practice.
But this is not really so strange as it seems; for to
those rebels respectability comes so easily that they
see no reason why they should make a virtue of it,

and they assume that those who do make a virtue of it have no other virtues to boast of. Indeed, it is because they do not think respectability a virtue that they have given to the word its present peculiar meaning.

Respectable, in the eighteenth century, meant worthy of respect. Then it was applied to the " deserving poor," and respectability became their main virtue from the point of view of the rich. It meant that they worked hard and knew their place, and were clean, honest, and sober; in fact, that they had all the qualities which made them useful to the well-to-do. Now these qualities are virtues, no doubt, but they are virtues that one would mention in a servant rather than in a friend. No one would say that he liked a man because he was respectable; he might describe a cook or a gardener in those terms to some one who asked for their character, but he would not recommend an equal so : he would not say, " You will like So-and-so, he is so respectable." Thus the word acquired a slightly patronising meaning, and we speak of a respectable performance when we mean that it is painstaking but mediocre.

But respectability, applied to people rather than to their performances, has lost even this amount of slighting commendation. It means no longer a real but an imitation virtue. The respectable are those whom no one respects, not even themselves, for they have not the power of respecting anything for its own sake. They practise certain virtues, perhaps, but they deserve no credit for them, since they practise

53

them only because other people think them virtues.
They have made rules for themselves in life, or rather
they have not made them, but have accepted them
at second hand. In a great part of their outward
conduct they behave like good men, but there is
nothing of the beauty or inspiration of goodness in
their behaviour, because there is no passion or conviction in it.

The good man pursues his own line of conduct, even
though the world thinks it evil, because he himself,
quick to hear the voice of conscience, knows that it
is good for him. In most things he may agree with
the world about what is right or wrong ; but this
agreement is a mere accident to him, whereas to the
respectable it is the essence of virtue. To them, if
the world chose to reverse the Ten Commandments,
the new ones would have all the prestige and authority
of the old. The moral commands and inhibitions are
rules for them, and if anyone breaks them he must
take the consequences ; which means that he will no
longer have the pleasure of their acquaintance, and
that not because they really hate his evil-doing, but
because, if they remained his friends, they might be
suspected of doing likewise. Saints do not judge
men much by their outward conduct, for they know
that the mind is often mistranslated by that ; but
the respectable judge by nothing else, since their
own natural conduct is everything to them, and,
while they keep the rules, they never ask themselves
why they do so.

In our orderly society it is often possible for the

prosperous to go through life without ever being tested in the essential virtues. Nothing happens to them to prove whether they are brave or cowards, whether, at a pinch, they would sacrifice themselves or some one else. They avoid the ruinous vices; but they do not know themselves—perhaps even their wives do not know—whether the high virtues are in them. Most of us are in this case, and it is well, therefore, that we should feel a general insecurity about our moral state.

In our ordinary lives there is more habit than will in our decent behaviour. Would our wills act rightly and imperiously, we may ask ourselves, if we were called upon to die for a cause with the whole world reviling it, or, harder still, to live for it ? That is a question which the respectable never put to themselves, if their virtue is merely respectability. For them the cause would be bad, if the world reviled it ; for them sufficient for the day is the good thereof, and the policeman takes the place of the categorical imperative. That is why they irritate others no less respectable in outward conduct. For these others feel that this outward respectability is no test of themselves ; they are insecure about their own virtue, and they despise the comfortable security of the respectable. Even the lost and ruined have faced the uttermost facts about themselves. They know how far they can sink, and how they can endure loneliness and shame. They have been tested, and it may be that to themselves there remains some pure spirit, after the test, of which they are utterly sure. But the rest of us have no right to be sure of any virtue of our own ; and the more sure we are, the less we deserve the comfort of our security.

ON BEING A GENTLEMAN

WE often talk of a born gentleman ; but gentlemen, like poets, have to make themselves, even when they have the best of material to deal with. There is no man worse-mannered than he who thinks that he knows how to be a gentleman by nature, that he has inherited good manners as if they were a title. He is different from the man who tries to be a gentleman the wrong way, and his failure is not so patent because he is making no effort. We do not laugh at him as we laugh at the other ; but we dislike him even more, and a man who is generally disliked may be sure that he has not succeeded in being a gentleman. For the peculiar virtues of a gentleman are æsthetic virtues— they are the virtues that give pleasure to others; and, if he has vices, they are not the vices that we hate instinctively. A gentleman is not the same as a saint, although a perfect saint would be a perfect gentleman, as the greater includes the less. But, as we are all imperfect, there is in practice a great difference between the saint and the gentleman, and a man may be very much of a gentleman without being at all a saint, just as there are men far advanced in sanctity whom no one would praise as gentlemen.

Modern Essays

John the Baptist was a saint, but he would not have
been praised as a gentleman either at the Court of
Herod or by those to whom he preached in the wilderness, and Julius Cæsar was, among the great men of
history, conspicuously a gentleman, but no one, except
Froude, would call him a saint. Yet the virtues of a
gentleman are not merely conventional signs of a
certain class ; they are real virtues, not social virtues
and those which we prize most in our ordinary relations
with each other.

A man may be a gentleman without being a Christian at all, as we confess when we speak of a Christian
and a gentleman. The two go very well together,
but they can only do that because they are different.
The Christian has a religious belief in the equality of
men because they all have immortal souls. The gentleman may not believe that they have immortal souls
at all, and he may have a profound disbelief in their
equality. Compared with the Christian, he is prosaic
in his relations with mankind ; his effort is not to
love them, because he believes that they are all part
of the glory of the universe, but to get on well with
them without stupid contentions or an ugly assertion
of his own dignity.

What Horace said of Aristippus fits the gentleman
very well. He is at his ease everywhere and with
everyone, and they are at ease with him. For he
knows enough about life to test his success not by his
own ease, but by theirs. Indeed, it is his virtue that
he can only enjoy his own ease by making others easy
with him. He may be selfish in many things, but

57

he is not an egotist, for egotism is an ugly vice and one that makes life difficult for the egotist. To the gentleman, unlike the Christian, nothing may be very important; but among all the other unimportant things he includes himself and his own affairs. For him, whatever the ultimate nature of the universe may be, there is a duty, which is also a pleasure, to make the best of it; and this best consists in a pleasant relation with other men, whether they be wise or foolish, great or lowly. He does not judge men by their station or by report; he likes to find out about them for himself, and he knows that he can only do that by a quick and easy intimacy, by manners free from all the conventions and pedantries of the socially insecure. He is never upon his dignity, for dignity to him is a by-product, something that you attain to if you know how to behave yourself, but not something that you can acquire by insisting upon it. It is, in fact, given to you by other men, not by yourself, and they will only give it to you if you do not seem to claim it.

As a finished product, the gentleman seems to do everything very easily; but that ease, like the ease of the habit, can only come by effort. He is socially secure; but, whatever his station, he was not born so, for no man ever is socially secure by birth, even if he was born to be a king. The test of a gentleman is the pleasure others take in his society, and not in his wit or his virtue or his learning, but in their ordinary social relations with him. And this pleasure he cannot give merely by being on good terms with himself.

Modern Essays

Darcy, in *Pride and Prejudice*, at least before Elizabeth took him in hand, could have given no pleasure
by his society to any one except the admiring Bingley.
No doubt he thought he was born a gentleman ; but
when he sulked in a ballroom he was only displaying
his social clumsiness. Shyness may account for his
bad manners, but they were bad manners all the
same, and the complete gentleman is not shy.

On this point we in England have a heresy at which
foreigners laugh, and which encourages us in our bad
manners. We think that the complete gentleman
may be shy, and we are indulgent to shyness even in
middle age. The French are not ; they think that it
is a man's social duty to overcome shyness, that he
has no right to be an oaf even because he thinks poorly
of himself. But we, because it is better to be shy
than blatant, make a virtue of shyness. And yet the
shy man may be a passive gentleman, but he is not
an active one. You may find him very delightful
if you draw him out ; but the active gentleman draws
you out and makes you feel that you are more of a
social success than you had ever suspected.

This is a very real virtue in him, even though it be
one that he could not have acquired without ease
and leisure. You may call it a class virtue, therefore ;
but everyone of his class does not possess it, and he
would not possess it if he had not made the most
of his opportunities. He is, socially, an artist ; and
he could not be that unless he had the disinterestedness of an artist, unless he admired, for their own
sake, the qualities which he has acquired. At any

59

rate, no man can become a gentleman because he hopes to get on by doing so. He may get on ; but his efforts to be a gentleman will only make people remark all the more that he is not one, just as they say of the successful charlatan that he is not an artist.

CHILDISHNESS

MAN, whatever else he has done, has never yet adapted himself to that struggle for life which is supposed to be his main business on earth. He is continually forced into it, but always absent-minded about it ; and it is in fits of absence of mind that he does the things of which he is most proud. Nor do we at all admire or like those men who have adapted them-selves most thoroughly to the struggle for life. It is true that biographies of them are written which insist that they are all they should be ; but in spite of those biographies we forget them as soon as we can. We choose rather to remember some one notorious for his forgetfulness of the struggle for life, some one who, as we say, was a child in matters of the world and who managed, in verse or prose, to express his determined childishness for our everlasting delight.

You cannot write poetry about your success in the struggle for life ; but you can write it about those things which have made you care nothing for it, about such trifles as the dew that sat in Julia's hair or such unrealities as the land of dreams, beyond the light of the morning star; and those things, if you have the gift for them, may remain familiar to many generations. Indeed there is a longer life for mere childish jingles like "Hush-a-by baby on the tree-top" than for the memory of any man who ever made a fortune by strict application to business. Sir Richard Whittington, it is true, did that and is still remembered; but it is because he had a cat and because he heard the bells saying, "Turn again, Whittington," not because he became Lord Mayor of London.

The child comes into the world ready to think of anything rather than the struggle for life; and this irrelevance of his delights us even when we have been subdued ourselves into complete relevance. All the queer unworldly mistakes of children not only amuse but charm us, for they set us remembering wistfully the time when we ourselves could make them. We still enjoy the story of Whittington, because he rose to fame and fortune not through his industry but through his cat, and because he was one to whom the bells could sing a song. They sang songs for us when we were children; and the world then was a place in which things might happen to us as they happened to Whittington—a place in which cats might talk and flowers had faces and children might come out of the pictures on the wall and play with us, and wonderful things happened in the garden at night, and always beyond the hills that we could see from our nursery window. We had learnt nothing then about cause and effect, and how they make the unexpected merely disagreeable. We might not believe in magic or fairies ; but there was no need to believe in them, for what we saw and did was just as wonderful as anything could be that we never saw or did. Indeed, it may be that all the stories of magic and fairies are only efforts made by men to prolong their childish wonder when they grow up. They cannot find it any longer in what is familiar, so they try to believe in another unfamiliar life all about them but unseen. It is not the children who make fairy stories, but the grown-ups. They people the flowers with those little imaginary creatures because the flowers themselves no longer have faces for them, as the bells say no words. And they tell their stories to the children because they want to see some one believe them ; but the children neither believe nor disbelieve. For them there need be nothing beyond the flowers themselves and the places where they know to find them.

Yet there are people who keep their childhood all their lives without trying to believe in fairies. They are not fools or under any illusion about the nature of things that the rest of us can detect ; and, if they are irrelevant as regards the struggle for life, they seem to have a relevance of their own, which we recognise even if we do not know its subject. And we recognise it because we remember it from our own childhood, when there was much more relevance in life for us than there is now. For in our hearts we all believe the struggle for life to be irrelevant ; and when Mozart, or any other of the unsubdued children, calls us away from it with his songs, we listen even if we do not follow; and we know that he, for all his carelessness, has a more serious business than our own. For in the music of these children there is both seriousness and carelessness; and they laugh, not at things, but with them. There is no bitterness in their laughter, for what they dislike they forget. And this they can do because the flowers have not lost their faces for them, or the bells their speech, because all the things that can be loved are alive to them, and the others are dead.

We cannot understand how Mozart got all his music out of life; but if we were still children we should understand, for then, if we had had his gift, we too could have turned everything to music, even our sorrows that came and went like rain on a June night; and after them there was more scent in the garden than before. He could weep, as he could laugh, better than anyone else; for sorrow meant something to him as much as laughter and everything meant something, except that irrelevance of the struggle for life which insists to us that it is the only relevant thing.

MEANNESS AND ITS MOTIVE

THERE is something heroic about miserliness. The names of famous misers go down in history, and the schoolboy in us thrills to the thought of a miser on the grand scale. He is picturesque; he may be amusing; at least he is thorough. His passion for gold is a great passion; he follows heroically and at great cost his purpose to amass it. But meanness over money matters has nothing great about it, and it is chiefly annoying because it seems to have no purpose except to be annoying.

Each one of us must have a friend or two who is afflicted with meanness. " As you are going that way, would you mind getting me a couple of stalls for the opera on Wednesday ? I'll send you a cheque "— and the cheque does not come. " Do be an angel and send this telegram for me as you pass the Post Office. I don't know how many words they'll make of the address, so I'll pay you when you tell me." Or perhaps it is, " You pay now, and we'll have a settling-up later."

We are all used to remarks of this kind—from male lips quite as often as from female ; and every time that we hear them, we wonder how people can be so mean. It seems so unlike their " real " characters. Very often they are people who are, in their own way, generous. They give good dinners and good presents ; they keep hospitable country-houses and " do you very well." And yet they will (to put it bluntly) swindle you out of a guinea or a sixpence which they could easily afford. The reason is not carelessness or forgetfulness ; if it were that, they would behave differently on the rare occasions when they are boldly asked to pay their debts. It is not the miser's love of saving and amassing and possessing gold : if it were that, they would never have allowed themselves

to come among circumstances which might subject
them to expense.

The motive seems to be a kind of distorted love of
superiority. If they can make you pay, be it only a
penny, they feel that they have worsted you, that
they are the stronger. That is why, when they are
cornered and flatly asked for the money, they betray
annoyance : it is you now who are stronger than
they. And they try to keep you under with a little
sneer, as if they were surprised at anyone troubling
about so paltry a sum. That, too, is why the whole
affair is so galling. They have counted, you know
very well, on the weakness in yourself, and have taken
it for granted that you are among those whom pride
or carelessness makes feeble. They inform you,
without words, that they think you a fool—the sort
of person with whom one can do anything, because
he is too timid, or too proud, or too impractical to
look after himself. And their joy is not in saving a
guinea, but in seeing you throw one away.

Well, their meanness is very petty and annoying ;
but they are not alone to blame. In the first place,
if the lender is foolish enough not to ask for his money
back, the borrower is indeed the stronger man of
the two and deserves his petty triumph. The motives
of the lender who never asks for his due may be
mixed, but all the ingredients in them are really bad.
There may be carelessness about money, which is
merely stupid ; there may be pride, which is pride
of the wrong sort, a pretence at being above such
considerations when all the while the affair is rank-

ling; there may be timidity, a fear of giving offence, which is at once the most contemptible and the most pernicious of the three. And, further, the borrower's action concerns his own morals alone; if he is mean, that is his own look-out. But the enforced lender who neglects to ask for his money back is giving another a lift on the road to perdition. The mean would soon be cured of their meanness if each one of their victims followed the plain duty of seeing that the trick failed; whereas every sixpence left unclaimed is another nail in the coffin of the mean man's honesty. On the sound principle that it is more virtuous to sin yourself than to be the cause of sin in others, the real culprit in these cases is the supine lender. And it is no excuse to say that his fault is a more agreeable fault than that of petty meanness.

ANTICIPATION AND MEMORY

WE are often told that the pleasures of anticipation are the greatest, as if life were therefore as deceitful as a mirage. But what a thing to be grateful for, that to the pleasure of the moment should be added this pleasure of expecting it. Anticipation, though it looks to the future, is really fed from the past. If we had nothing in our experience to go by, we could expect nothing. Our ideas of heaven itself are made out of the most heightened moments of our lives, with that further heightening that the mind can give to past experience which it throws forward into the future. Light, music, space, the sense of power in glorious companionship, the surprise of good news better than we had ever dreamt of, the rolling away of all trouble of mind and body as if it were only an April storm that made the sunshine brighter—all these things we have known more or less in this life; and we can combine them in imagination so that each gives tenfold power to the rest.

> " Where the bright Seraphim in burning row
> Their loud uplifted angel trumpets blow ;
> And the Cherubic host in thousand choirs
> Touch their immortal harps of golden wires."

Milton made these lines out of his own memories of music ; and the flight of angels in the paradises of the painters is remembered from the wings of great birds flashing white in the infinite space of the sky.

If we expect more than we get of delight, it is because memory also heightens delight, purifying it from the anxiety and from all the little abatements of the present. But it does more than that, for our minds have a spell that they cast over their own past experiences, so that we can all be artists or poets when we remember. We may not at the moment be aware that we see in the delightful thing something that is still itself, only better ; but in memory this further something takes the place of the reality, keeping its vividness and authenticity, yet glorified as if it were the version of a great painter ; and it is these versions of the past that we expect to be our actual experience

Modern Essays

in the future. They never are, perhaps, or only when some surprise of delight comes to us like a dream without anticipation; but it is not fair therefore to talk of life as if it were all jam yesterday and jam to-morrow but never jam to-day. For memory and anticipation, though they deal with past and future, are themselves in the present; and those who say that they are mere illusions provided by nature, whatever nature may be, to keep us in conceit with living, talk so because they have never learnt how to make use of them.

For it may be that they tell us the truth about things, and that it is some blindness in us which prevents us from seeing that truth when it is before our eyes. There is an illusion somewhere, but it may be the illusion of the disturbing moment itself, that we can overcome if we will make the experiment of distrusting it. Of course, if you believe with Hamlet in his distemper that there is nothing either good or bad but thinking makes it so, you will never be able to protect your mind against its own ups and downs; but no one ever really believes that, except when thinking seems to make everything bad. When things are good to us they seem to us good in themselves, and our egotism loses itself in our sense of their goodness. This egotism, which, like an aching tooth, makes everything seem unreal except its own pain, hinders present delight; but afterwards we forget our egotism and remember the delightful thing; and so too in anticipation we expect the delightful thing, but not the recurrence of our egotism.

68

Therefore we can make the experiment of believing what memory and anticipation tell us about things, rather than what the troubled egotism of the moment tells us; and we can train ourselves, even at the moment, to see things as we see them when we remember or expect them. Indeed, to do this is the achievement of the mystic. He believes that the heightened significance and glory of things is not a trick of his own mind, but the true reality which the mind can only receive as still waters take a reflection. He has the power of stilling his mind at the moment with a reverence for reality outside himself, but for most of us it is only stilled by memory or anticipation. We remember the broken reflections as if they were perfect, and we expect them to be perfect again, and so it is only the past and the future that tell us what the present might be.

DIFFERENCES OF TASTE

THOUGHT is strangely at the mercy of words, and is constantly confused by the use of words in different senses. There is no better instance of this than the different uses of the word taste. When we say that there is no disputing about tastes, we use the word to mean those instinctive, unaccountable preferences which in themselves are neither good nor bad and are not subject to any control of the will. One man prefers hock to claret, another claret to hock. One man likes red hair and another dislikes it. One man chooses to spend his holiday upon the mountains and another on the sea. Each of these likes and dislikes is indeed a matter of taste, not of good or bad taste. No man is to be praised or blamed for any of them, and there is no means of proving that any of them is either right or wrong. In fact, they are neither right nor wrong.

But when we speak of good or bad taste, we are using the word in a different sense altogether—using it of those likes and dislikes into which the will enters, and which can be, and ought to be, affected by training. Yet it is often of these tastes that people speak when they say there is no disputing about tastes. They think they are repeating a truism, but by altering the meaning of the word taste they are really making a new and most disputable statement—namely, that there is no such thing as good or bad taste, no likes and dislikes that are, or ought to be, affected by training and subject to principles. Instead of saying that it is all one whether a man prefers hock to claret or claret to hock, they are saying that it is all one whether a man prefers good hock to bad, or bad to good.

This is evidently an absurd proposition, because bad food and drink disagree with us, and we know when they do so. But the absurdity is not so evident when the proposition relates to other matters where the effects of goodness and badness are not so plain and immediate. A man may have the worst possible taste in literature or art and yet suffer no pain in his inside.

Indeed, he may never be aware of any evil results from
his bad taste. We cannot even be sure that he enjoys
bad things less than a man of good taste enjoys good
ones.

Some people fall into raptures over the pictures of
Ary Scheffer, and are thoroughly comfortable in a
room entirely decorated with *l'art nouveau :* and such
people often appear to be suffering from no kind of
moral corruption, and are indeed not guilty even of
bad taste in their conduct. That is the reason why
it is sometimes contended that there is no good or
bad taste in art, or at least that nobody's taste can
be, or needs to be, affected by training. A man says,
" I know what I like," implying that that is all he
needs to know about the matter, that there is no need
for him to give or to be aware of reasons why he likes
it. He is a law to himself, or rather he is subject to
no law that can be discovered. If he prefers Ary
Scheffer to Titian, it is as if he preferred hock to claret.
He was born so, and any effort on his part to change
his preference would prove him guilty of weakness
or insincerity.

This view implies, of course, that there is no more
in art than in hock or claret ; that the enjoyment of
art is a mere pleasure of the senses, like the enjoyment
of meat and drink. Directly we assume that art expresses anything, we must admit that there are differences of value in what is expressed in it. We make
this admission readily enough about literature. Any
one can see that what is expressed by Shakespeare has
more value than what is expressed by Tupper. It

is clear indeed that Tupper does not succeed in expressing anything at all with any precision. He tries
to say weighty things, but achieves nothing except
a weighty manner. Therefore to prefer Tupper to
Shakespeare is merely to be deceived by him. It is
not the result of taste at all, but only of inexperience.

It is not so easy to prove this in other arts, because
we can only prove it in words, and words are not their
means of expression. But, if pictures and music, like
poetry, express anything, there must be differences of
value in what they express; and in some cases they
too are likely to express nothing in particular, and to
be mere vague imitations of other works that are really
expressive. It is a mark of bad taste to be taken in
by these, to prefer the imitation to the original, or a
vague to a precise expression; and bad taste of this
kind is very common, though no one can be convicted
of it by any logical process.

Vague, imitative, and sentimental things have their
day, and while it lasts are often more popular than
masterpieces, because there is some timidity or laziness
in the human mind that dislikes what is precise and
original. But that day does not last long. Bad
taste is usually deceived only by the frauds of its own
time. It can laugh at its own mistakes in the past,
though it will not learn from them; and it pays respect
to old masterpieces, however much it may dislike new
ones. It is always changing, and for that reason is
never convicted by the judgment of posterity. The
man who admires certain living authors who need not
be mentioned is not aware that if he had been born

two generations back he would have admired Tupper ;
and he will probably be dead when his favourite books
are also as dead as the *Proverbial Philosophy*.   Meanwhile, if any one tells him that his favourite books
are bad, he says that there is no disputing about
tastes, meaning that his taste is as good as anyone
else's.   It is not ; but since no one can prove that,
he remains content with it.

BAD TASTE IN CONDUCT

THERE is a very strong tendency among us nowadays,
so strong and so instinctive that we are scarcely aware
of it, to judge conduct, as the Greeks judged it, by
æsthetic as well as moral standards ; or, rather, to
regard the æsthetic and the moral standard as the
same.   The Greeks implied a moral judgment when
they said that an action was beautiful or ugly ; and
people have assumed that they did so because they
had not yet learned to distinguish between beauty and
goodness.   But we, who once seem to have thought
that they had nothing in common, are approaching
more and more to the Greek opinion that they are
closely connected ; and if a proof of this is needed it
is to be found in our modern use of the words " good "
and " bad " taste.

These words used only to be applied to what we still
call matters of taste.   There was good or bad taste in
wine or pictures, or furniture or dress.   But now we

constantly speak of good or bad taste in matters of conduct, and we pass a moral judgment when we do so. It is true that the words still have a trivial sound, because taste used to be considered a trivial matter; but they no longer have a trivial meaning, as anyone can prove for himself. Tell a man that something he has said or done was in very bad taste, and he will resent it as much as if you called him a liar. It is easy to sneer at this modern insistence upon the importance of good taste; and the words may of course be used in a narrow and conventional way. We used to think of taste as something quite arbitrary, having no connection with character or intellect; and if we keep that view of it when we speak of good or bad taste in conduct, we have no right to attribute any importance to it. But the fact that we do speak of good and bad taste in conduct proves that we no longer regard taste as arbitrary. It proves that we are becoming more and more aware of that connection between beauty and goodness which seemed so close to the Greeks, that like them we are learning to judge of the motives of an action by the manner in which it is performed.

For we are always concerned with manner when we speak of good or bad taste in conduct; and when we resent the bad taste of an action, what we resent in it is the manner of performance. In doing so we apply an artistic standard of judgment; for a work of art is judged entirely by the manner in which it is performed, and we do not estimate an artist either by his motives or by any non-artistic effect of his work.

Modern Essays

A man may write a poem with some excellent moral purpose, and it may produce the effect which he desires; but, in spite of that, if the poem is badly written, we do not call him a good poet. Now it may be argued that we have no right to apply this kind of artistic judgment to matters of conduct. In the ordinary actions of life a man does not pretend to be an artist, and it is unjust to treat him as if he were one. But the answer is that we are only aware of bad taste in conduct when there is some artistic intention in it, when it makes some appeal to the emotions and makes it badly. However brutal a man may be, however ruthless or selfish, his actions are not in bad taste if they are performed quite simply and without any attempt to conceal their character by incongruous excuses. Napoleon only fell into bad taste when he played to the gallery, when he tried to justify his actions by the display of emotions which he did not feel, by an appeal to sentiments for which he had no respect. Then he tried to be an artist, and was a bad one, and so subjected himself to an artistic judgment. In a vast number of actions we display no kind of taste, good or bad, for we make no kind of emotional appeal in our performance of them; and any man can escape the imputation of bad taste if he will perform all his actions quite simply, without asking himself how they will affect other people's opinions of him and without trying to produce effects not proper to them.

We dislike bad taste in conduct because it is the result of the same kind of emotional insincerity that disgusts us in bad art. Just as we condemn a bad artist because there is no reason why he should try to be an artist at all, so we condemn bad taste in conduct because it seems to us entirely gratuitous, because it is trying to be good taste. In fact, it adds insult to injury, for we are insulted when a man tries to deceive us by incongruous appeals to our emotions, and we dislike him more for the insult to our intelligence than for any real injury he may do us.

This insult exists even when no injury is done, when conduct that is in bad taste is not wrong in itself. For a man who makes any kind of appeal to us in bad taste assumes that our taste is the same as his own; and we are vexed with a strong desire to prove that it is not. This is the cause of that extreme discomfort we experience when any one makes a joke in bad taste and looks round for approval. Then we feel that we shall seem to be his accomplices unless we show our disapproval; yet often we cannot show it. It is far more difficult to protest against bad taste than against actual wrong-doing; for how is one to prove that it is bad? A man may do a wrong act and see that it is wrong, and his better nature may cause him to regret it at once. But bad taste is the product of a man's whole nature; if he could see that it was bad he would not be guilty of it. He makes his gross, or vulgar, or incongruous appeal because it is the kind of appeal that would move him if some one else made it. And that is why our æsthetic resentment against bad taste is also a moral resentment. Since it is the product of a man's whole nature, our whole nature is exasperated and estranged by it with an emotional estrangement which is far wider and more instinctive than any estrangement caused by reason alone.

We often have to harden our minds against a mere evil-doer, and to persuade ourselves, as it were, to dislike him. But our difficulty with a man who shows gross bad taste in his conduct is to refrain from disliking him more than he deserves. If he has good qualities, they seem to us accidental. His bad taste taints everything he does, like a nasty flavour in food ; in fact, it seems to be the man himself, and, when we hate it, we find it hard not to hate him also.

TASTE AND ITS STANDARDS

Is there any criterion of right and wrong in matters of taste ? The average man would probably answer without hesitation in the negative. " Every one to his taste," he would say. The saying has passed into a proverb which has its counterpart in other languages. And yet, if we reflect a little, we must fain acknowledge that criticism of all kinds implies as its fundamental postulate that in matters of taste there is such a thing as right and wrong, just as there is in morals.

It is true that criticism has often proved to be wrong in its deliverances, as when Keats was bidden " back to his gallipots," and Jeffrey wrote petulantly

of Wordsworth " This will never do." But the very
fact that these early judgments have been by common
consent reversed proves only that criticism, especially
contemporary criticism, is not infallible, and at least
implies, if it does not prove, that there is such a thing
as right and wrong in matters of taste. In point of
fact, however strongly a man may claim to be anti-
nomian in matters of taste, if he prefers such a picture
as Frith's " Derby Day " to any of the masterpieces
of Titian, Raphael, or Velasquez; if he prefers a
modern musical comedy to *As You Like It*, or a
trumpery melodrama to such a tragedy as *Hamlet*
or *Othello;* if he prefers a commonplace piece of
popular music to a Concerto of Bach or a Symphony
of Beethoven; even if, in respect of the pleasures of
sense, he prefers a glass of gin and water to the finest
growths of the Côte d'Or, the Gironde, or the Rhine—
we should all agree that he is a man of indifferent
taste, and in nine cases out of ten he would probably
say the same himself.

Or—to take another illustration from the apprecia-
tion of natural scenery—there has lately been some
discussion in certain quarters as to whether Humboldt
was right in pronouncing a certain view in the Island
of Teneriffe on the road between Santa Cruz and
Orotava to be the finest view in the world. Here
individual predilection would seem to come in at its
highest. There is nothing about which men differ so
much as about the beauty of different kinds of natural
scenery. Yet merely to raise the question implies
that there is some canon or criterion to which all men

of good taste would defer, and by which, if once recognised and established, they would all agree to abide.

It may be argued that the question is begged by saying " all men of good taste." But that is not really so. We all acknowledge that, in matters of conduct, there is a definite standard of right and wrong. But although this abstract standard of morals is recognised as supreme and indefeasible, yet even here there are many concrete cases and questions about which good men might well feel a difficulty as to the right course of conduct to pursue. Aristotle long ago pointed out that in such cases the only criterion is the judgment of the right-thinking man, of the man whose habitual right conduct has endowed him with a right judgment. The same idea is expressed in more spiritual fashion by the canon of the Gospel, " If any man will do His will, he shall know of the doctrine." It is true that a perversion of this doctrine has given rise to the so-called science of casuistry, and casuistry has no good repute among right-thinking men. But there is a sound casuistry as well as an unsound; and no man can be said to have had a very wide ethical experience if his own conscience has never been confronted with a concrete conflict between right and right in the abstract.

In like manner in the domain of taste, which is a much less important and less explored field than that of morals, there is a sphere within which the standard of good and bad taste is fixed and irrevocable, surrounded by a much larger sphere in which the standard is much more flexible and indeterminate. Thus the

analogy between taste and morals seems to be a
very close one, except that, for obvious reasons, the
sphere in which the absolute standard operates without serious question is much larger in the domain of
conduct than it is in that of taste. Every man must
recognise some standard of conduct if he is to live
at peace with his neighbours, and indeed with himself.
But whether he should also have a sound standard of
taste is a question which mainly concerns himself.
Yet it is hardly too much to say that, if it had been
as important to the affairs and relations of men to
have a right standard in taste as it is to have a right
standard in conduct, there might long ago have been
as large and general a consensus in matters of taste as
there has long been in matters of morals.

How, then, are we to determine what is right or
wrong in matters of taste? Here the analogy of morals
helps us again. Just as in difficult questions of morals
the right-thinking man—the man whose conduct has
enlightened his judgment, and whose judgment, so
enlightened, has in turn refined his conduct—is best
fitted to decide, so in matters of taste the man of
good taste is also best fitted to decide. Good taste
is partly an inborn gift, and partly one that may, and
indeed must, be cultivated by practice and study.
Just as there are men born with a native bias towards
virtue, so there are men born with a native gift of
good taste. But in each case practice and the study
of great examples are needed to refine and perfect the
native gift. It is therefore no complete theory of
taste to say that, although there is a general consensus

in matters of right and wrong, yet in matters of taste
there is no such thing, that tastes vary from age to
age, that that which delights one generation fails
even to attract the next, and that even the best
of critics sometimes make egregious mistakes. The
answer is that some things delight all generations,
that critics are all agreed on certain points, and that
these are the materials on which all good taste must
be based. All critics are agreed, for example, that
Homer, Sophocles, Virgil, Dante, and Shakespeare
are among the greatest poets of the world ; and any
man who disputes that judgment is manifestly out of
court. *Securus judicat orbis terrarum.*

The judgment of the world, rectified and refined from
generation to generation, is final and brooks no appeal.
Contemporary judgments, even those of critics of
high repute, are often false, misguided, and misleading.
But in the case of the great creations of the human
spirit, whether in literature, art, or music, all criticism
which is shallow, ephemeral, capricious, or perverse
is slowly dissolved away by time, and there is left
the pure gold of universal and undisputed apprecia-
tion. It is thus only by the study of the great creations of the human spirit that an unimpeachably good
taste can be acquired. That is the best corrective of
antinomianism in taste, just as the study of high
thoughts, and the contemplation of noble deeds, are
among the strongest safeguards against antinomianism
in morals.

MIND AND CIRCUMSTANCE

A WAR correspondent once remarked how the whole
of the superficial luxuries of civilisation seem to disappear in a twinkling the moment one crosses the
frontier into any kingdom where war is taking place.
Moreover, you feel no surprise at the change ; you
accept everything as if things had always been so.
So adaptable a creature is man. But this adaptability
in most men is subject to one condition. They must
be prepared for the change before it happens, and
they must feel that there is a good reason for it. We
can all make up our minds to endure something on a
special occasion when we are prepared for it ; and
often the effort is so much greater than what we have
to endure that the actual moment of endurance passes
almost unnoticed, and after it we laugh joyfully at
ourselves for our own expense of heroism.   Our spirits
are like stocks and shares, which fall so much in expectation of some calamity that they rise as soon as
the calamity has happened. But this kind of adaptability, given to us by Nature, is, like most natural
gifts, uncertain and wasteful in its action. The
problem is to develop it into a higher kind of adaptability, not wasteful and not at the mercy of surprise.

There are many old maxims designed to encourage
that kind of adaptability in us. " Every cloud has a
silver lining," " It is a long lane that has no turning,"
" Nothing is half so bad as it seems." But the worst

of these is that they seem platitudes while we prosper, and lies at the moment of disaster. They are like simple household remedies which may or may not be of some use for a cold in the head, but which are of no use whatever for an attack of double pneumonia. And as in a serious illness it is the constitution and the whole habit of life which tells, so in a serious calamity we have to rely on the constitution of the mind and general habits of conduct and thought. The mind will adapt itself to the worst disasters, and react into happiness or tranquillity after them, if only it can recover from the first shock.

What it needs is something to protect it from the shock. It needs not merely a general knowledge that disasters may occur, but, as it were, a plan of campaign and an organisation ready at any moment to deal with them. That is something entirely different from those vague apprehensions which spoil the security of so many prosperous people. We cannot train ourselves to bear disaster by thinking of all the particular disasters that might happen to us. To do that produces a habit of panic, not of preparation; and we can never prepare in detail for every disaster that may come. Nor can we steel ourselves against a possible sorrow by refusing to enjoy any actual joy. For joy increases the health of the mind, and so strengthens it against the attacks of sorrow. In joy we forget ourselves; and self-forgetfulness is the best possible habit for the mind to acquire. Indeed, if we can acquire it so as to maintain it through all changes of circumstance, we have learnt complete adaptability and the secret of life. For if we can forget ourselves in discomfort or disaster, those things do not exist for us. Nietzsche has remarked that the martyr rejoices in the moment of torture, not because he can endure it, but because he finds that there is nothing to endure. He has forgotten himself so completely in his faith that there remains no self for the persecutor to take hold of.

So it is, to take a more commonplace example, with the eager and curious traveller who enters a country where war is being waged. He does not notice discomforts because he is interested, not in himself and his dinner-hour, but in the war. For that emergency he has learnt the secret of life, and is surprised at his own adaptability. But very likely, the first time he goes to his club after his return home, he grumbles because his chop is not exactly as he likes it, or because there is too much air, or too little, in the smoking-room. The cause of this returning sensitiveness to circumstances is lack of interest in them. So soon as we cease to be absorbed in things or people outside us we become absorbed in ourselves, and at the mercy of our own appetites and sensations. Boredom is the root of all egotism, and the mind when it is bored, like the body when its vitality is lowered, is susceptible to any disease that may attack it. Thus the secret of life is never to be bored. Put that way, it sounds trivial and prosaic enough. It is only when we consider how we are to escape boredom that we find it is not prosaic or trivial. For we can never escape it by fleeing from all the things that may bore us. Boredom

84

is a state of failure less acute than sorrow, but a symptom of the same trouble, namely, consciousness of self.

And this consciousness of self is increased by every effort we make at self-protection. If we are always guarding ourselves against boredom, it seems a serious calamity to be buttonholed by a bore. But if we can only interest ourselves in the psychology of the bore, he ceases to be one. We forget ourselves and our own discontent in studying him. So the traveller, from his interest in the war, forgets the discomforts which it causes to him. In fact, it is possible to transform the self from a passive thing which is at the mercy of particular discomforts to an active thing which subjects all circumstances to its own general purpose and uses them all as materials for that purpose. Happiness, as opposed to occasional and precarious joys, consists in this active power; which is a power of adapting, not the self to circumstances, but circumstances to the self.

And the paradox is that we only have this power when we forget ourselves in our purpose, whatever it may be. Without a purpose the self absorbs us, imperious but impotent, demanding everything and content with nothing, like a hungry babe that will not be soothed with toys. But give it a purpose, and it sinks into contentment like an infant put to the breast. The only difficulty is that, whereas we all know that mother's milk is the best food for babies, every man has to discover for himself what purpose is mother's milk for his soul.

85

Modern Essays

THE LATIN GENIUS

M. POINCAIRE, in a speech in praise of Leonardo delivered at the Sorbonne, said that Leonardo, artist and man of science, combined in a remarkable manner the peculiar qualities and gifts of the Latin nations, being both imaginative and practical in the highest degree. Certainly no Northerner has ever been as various in achievement as he was, has ever applied the same amount of intellect to so many different activities. Goethe came nearest to him in this respect, and he did so by a conscious effort, turning towards the south like a flower in a northern garden. But usually among Northern men of genius there is a sharp division between the imaginative and the practical. Powers are more specialised and curiosity is more limited. The Renaissance itself was Italian, and the Northern nations caught the contagion of it only for a time and misunderstood it even then.

For the Renaissance in Italy was not merely an attempt to revive the art or science of the ancient world. In its essence it was an attempt to live a new kind of life, and its art and science were only expressions of this attempt. The great artists of the Renaissance did not suppose, like the critics of the eighteenth century, that their forefathers had been mere clumsy barbarians in art. Their achievement, as they well knew themselves, was not to raise art from the dead, but to express in it a view of life quite different from the view held and expressed in the Middle Ages ; and this was the view of life natural to Southern peoples when free from the pressure of adversity. In fact, with the Renaissance the South came into its own again, and threw off Northern ideas just as it threw off the Gothic architecture of the North. It hailed the remains of the ancient world with a passion of delight because it recognised its own true self in them with a dream-like mixture of remembrance and discovery.

That Southern view of life, which was Greek as well as Latin, is, as M. Poincaré said, both imaginative and practical ; and its peculiar union of the two is very difficult for Northerners to understand, however much they may admire the results of it. For, to put it a little more precisely, the Northern imagination is stirred mainly by the unknown, the Southern by the known. Thus the Northerner makes a sharp division between realism and romance which the Southerner does not make ; and the natural tendencies of Northern and Southern art are entirely different. The whole artistic effort of the Renaissance was to express imagination through fact, and its art increased continually in fulness of representation ; but the artistic effort of the North is to express imagination with as little fact as possible. To a Northerner facts are prosaic ; and usually the more imagination he has, the more he is in love with the unseen. Thus the career of a great Northern artist like Rembrandt was in the opposite direction to the career of a great Southern artist like Leonardo. Rembrandt mastered facts as a necessary means of expression ; but, having mastered them, his whole effort was to eliminate them. Leonardo could satisfy himself with the effort to make his painting like reality, not because he was a prosaic imitator of facts, but because his imagination was satisfied with reality, or at any rate with its possibilities. The Northern mind is not satisfied even with the possibilities of reality. Its idea of heaven is one that no eye can see even in day dreams, that cannot be expressed by any concrete images taken from the visible world. So Northern imaginative painting is seldom a representation of beautiful things or people, for the beauty of the visible world will not satisfy a mind in love with the unknown. To Rembrandt, Christ as man is a God submitting to the burden of the flesh. To the great Italians of the Renaissance the flesh is not a burden, and the beauty of God and the angels can be adequately represented in it. Thus Northerners are apt to find something frivolous in the heaven of Correggio, the most Southern of all artists. But to a Southerner, being the visible world at its height of beauty, it is heaven. To him the unseen is the non-existent, and he is not interested in a heaven which does not exist.

The chief art of the North is music, an art entirely independent of imitation, which creates a world for itself and gets all its beauty not from the facts of reality but from the mind of its creator. In music the Northern artist can express all his desires without showing us what he desires, and in doing that he expresses also the Northern view of life, which seems mere misty foolishness to the Southerner. The

Southerner's effort is always to discover what he desires in the real world, for to him a desire is something that he wishes to satisfy. The Northerner, on the other hand, values a desire in proportion as it cannot be satisfied. He will not glorify instincts and appetites even if he yields to them. To him there is no such thing as a heaven of the senses, and man is Divine only in so far as he frees himself from the allurements of the flesh. But to the Southerner Divinity consists in the intensity and balance of all faculties, and the beauty of the flesh is part of it.

We are apt to be unjust to his view of life, because we know it best by its evil effects upon the Northern mind, to which it is often poison. An Italianised Englishman is often a devil incarnate, because the Southern view of life to him means only licence. He adopts it without its conscience, and it appeals to his appetites rather than to his imagination. The Renaissance in the North produced not Leonardos or Michelangelos, but bad imitators of the Borgias; and so there was a fierce Puritan reaction against it. But the true men of the Renaissance were preserved from excess by the diversity of their interests. They were not often saints, but they have enlarged our ideas of the capacity of the human mind; and, though we cannot accept the heaven which they offer to us, we must acknowledge that they came very near to realising it for themselves.

Modern Essays

THREATENING LETTERS AND WITCHCRAFT

WE have long ceased to believe in witchcraft, and when we read of the trials of supposed witches and the savage sentences that were passed upon them we are apt to think of them as instances of the unintelligible cruelty of our ancestors. Yet our ancestors were, we may be sure, men very like ourselves. The main difference between them and us in this matter of witchcraft was that they believed in it and we do not. Their belief caused them to commit much cruel injustice, but they did not commit it for the sake of doing so. They had to deal with a real and very serious evil, and often with real and very serious offences. It was their ignorance of the true nature of that evil and those offences that led them astray. We no longer try people for witchcraft, but we try them for offences which would probably in the seventeenth century have taken the form of pretended or supposed witchcraft; and we still recognise those offences to be serious.

A case in point occurred recently at the Bristol Assizes, where a man was tried for sending threatening letters and sentenced to nine months' imprisonment. The man was described as occasionally hysterical, and he appears to have suffered from some form of religious mania. He had been a member of the Catholic Apostolic Church, and having left that Church he conceived a grievance against the prosecutor, who was a

Bishop in it. The result was that he sent him letters and telegrams accusing him of unspecified villainies and threatening his life. This was not a case of blackmail. The prisoner had no aim except to gratify his grudge, and with that object he took the best means he could find of frightening his enemy.

It is still a criminal offence to do this, whether the author of a threat intends to carry it out or not. The law protects people not only against violence but against the fear of it, and rightly. But that fear of violence, which the prisoner in this case tried to instil, is nothing compared with the fears against which the laws dealing with witchcraft were directed. A man whose life is threatened can take measures to protect it. He can, as in this case, have the offender arrested. But no kind of material protection would avail against the spells of a witch, if a witch really had the power of casting them. We have only to conceive of ourselves as believing in witchcraft to understand why our ancestors killed witches. The danger from them was increased by their imprisonment, since that would naturally increase their malignance; it could be ended only by their death.

And this danger was one that affected the mind far worse than any threat of physical violence. We still hear of people in remote villages who complain of being overlooked, and who actually pine away under the belief that a spell has been cast upon them. There is a hypochondriac tendency in human nature which thrives best upon vague and mysterious fears. It was this tendency that made witchcraft so great a terror for those who believed in it. If once they thought they were under a spell, every little mischance, every slight disorder suffered by any member of their family, was taken as a proof that the spell was working. And upon minds so disposed the spell did work. We may well believe that people died and went mad from witchcraft. All through the later Middle Ages, that period of fantastic fears and mental epidemics, the belief in witchcraft grew and the evils caused by it became more real. Many innocent people were punished; but many were also punished who were not innocent, who believed in their own diabolical powers, and who did deadly injury to their enemies by what we now call the power of suggestion.

It appears that many of those who supposed themselves to be witches were insane, or at least hysterical; and no doubt the same disorder of mind made them also malignant. The desire to work upon the fears of others, whether it leads to the writing of threatening letters or to the uttering of mysterious curses, is in itself a morbid symptom. It is a mind exasperated by its own sense of weakness that desires power at all costs and by any means. Thus those who professed witchcraft were usually insignificant people, who evidently got little material profit by their wickedness; and probably it was this fact more than any other that destroyed the belief in witchcraft. When it became clear that witches were a miserable race, who might do harm to others, but could do no good to themselves, the theory spread that they were possessed by delusions instilled in them by the Devil. They were still supposed to be wicked, since their delusions were the penalty of their wickedness; but it was a wickedness that need be harmful only to themselves.

This was not quite true, but it was somewhere near the truth; and it led to our present understanding of the workings of morbid minds which, if still imperfect, has at least freed us from the contagion of such morbidity. When now a man conceives an irrational grudge against another man, and writes threatening letters to him, the victim is not wrought upon by superstitious fears. He may be in danger, but he knows exactly what that danger is and can deal with it. It may be difficult in particular cases to decide whether the offender should be treated as a criminal or as a lunatic, but either treatment will at least prevent him from doing further harm. In the times when he cast spells instead of writing threatening letters, there was no way of dealing with him except to kill him; and even then no one knew how long the spell would work. We can hardly wonder that he was often cruelly tortured so that he might be induced to recall his spells, for no punishment could seem too severe for the man who leagued with devils against his fellow-men.

SHYNESS AND HATRED

MAXIM GORKI sent a letter in reply to the congratulations of a number of Englishmen upon his play *The Lower Depths*, in which this saying occurs—" The world knows itself little; I think it is richer than it seems to us. Men know each other imperfectly; that is one reason why life seems to them so hard." This, no doubt, was a general reflection, yet it applies particularly to Englishmen and to the society of our time. For, through a strange kind of nervousness, we more than any other people raise obstacles against our knowledge of each other, and by doing so deprive ourselves of one of the greatest pleasures in life and of the chief means of understanding it.

We have ceased, perhaps, to pride ourselves upon our shyness, but we have not got rid of it. We are still afraid of strangers, and apt to assume their hostility, or at least their unlikeness, to ourselves. It is this fear that produces silence among us, or, where silence would be ill-mannered, that pretence of conversation called small-talk, in which every topic that could possibly interest any human intelligence is carefully avoided. And yet we all delight in a man who will set us at our ease, who is not afraid to give himself away, who assumes friendliness and intelligence and a general human likeness to himself in everyone that he meets. He by the mere warmth of his spirit will bring a crowd of Englishmen round him as if he were a fire and will melt their reserve, not only towards him, but towards each other. He makes life richer for them than they had ever supposed it to be, dissolving their unmeaning secrecies as the sun dissolves the mists.

But most of us, with regard to the great mass of men, live in a mist thrown out by our own minds,

through which all figures look dull and vague and distorted ; and we are not taught any system of thought
or conduct by which we can dispel that mist. Indeed,
many learn from their earliest youth to be on their
guard against their fellow-men, not so much from
suspicion as from false shame. It is the criticism
of strangers that they fear rather than their advances ;
and they will not make advances themselves lest they
should be ridiculed for doing so. They assume that
other men are unlike themselves until some accident
reveals the common likeness, and their whole life is
impoverished by this assumption.

For the teaching and experience of all the wisest
and happiest of mankind go to prove that there is
far more likeness than unlikeness between men, and
that wisdom and happiness are to be gained only by
assuming the likeness and acting upon that assumption. We all like ourselves except when we are
morbidly disposed ; and we like other people when
we find that they resemble ourselves. Then we pay
them the highest compliment we can by calling them
human, meaning thereby that in their very faults
they are like us, and therefore pardonable. But we
mean also, perhaps without knowing it, that they have
the power of revealing themselves in all that they do.
The man whom we call human is not ashamed or
afraid of his humanity in all its imperfections. He
does not wish to persuade anyone that he is different
from what he is ; and his frankness provokes frankness
in others, so that they reveal their humanity to him
without fear. He may be no genius ; but life for him

95

through his frankness and boldness is a voyage of discovery in which he gets to know far more of men merely by trusting them than the most brilliant of distrustful cynics.

On the other hand, we call a man inhuman when we see no likeness in him to ourselves ; and it is this sense of unlikeness that produces hatred. Where men seem to each other merely hostile mechanical forces, there is sure to be hatred between them, a hatred made the more intense by the mask of humanity which each seems to the other to wear. We do not hate a machine, but we hate a man who seems to behave like one ; and that is the reason for the common dislike of officials, who appear, when they thwart us, to be men set to play the part of machines. Then it is peculiarly difficult for us to remember that behind the official manner there is a man like ourselves, and that the official manner is assumed only that the man may protect himself against the blandishments of our humanity and against his own human weaknesses.

So in times of revolution some official has appeared to a furious mob a mere symbol of all the evil and oppression they wish to destroy. They forget his humanity altogether, and tear him in pieces as if he were a mere effigy of himself. So it was with Foulon in the French Revolution, and we may be sure that the mob were the less disposed to pity the victims of the Inquisition because of the hideous symbolic garments in which their humanity was concealed. Men clothed thus were not men but merely heretics ; and so it is that hatred always clothes its objects in an ugly garment of misunderstanding. But the misunderstanding usually exists before the hatred—a misunderstanding, not of particular men, but of all mankind. That seems to be born in all of us as a kind of primitive instinct, inherited, perhaps, from the time when every stranger was likely to be an enemy ; and it is one of those natural timidities which we need to overcome before we can call ourselves civilised, before we can be sure that we are altogether human and not still partly brutes.

THE VICTORIAN AGE

It is the fashion in these enlightened days for men of letters, publicists, critics, *et hoc genus omne*, to belittle the Victorian age and to represent it as humdrum, *bourgeois*, banal, Philistine, plentifully lacking in ideas, and sadly muddled in its handling of the few it laid hold of, conventional in sentiment, commonplace in taste, prim and puritanical in morals, in a word wholly inferior in all these respects to the age in which it is now our privilege to live.

Those who have lived through the Victorian age would not, we feel sure, recognise the portrait. It is a posthumous portrait, and the majority of those who have drawn it have never seen the original. There is no period of history in which the average man is so ignorant, or which he finds it so difficult to regard in a true perspective, as that which immediately preceded his own time. He can find very little of it in books, and his knowledge of it can never be equal to that of those who lived through it. He is conscious of a difference between his own ideas and those of his father and his father's contemporaries, he understands his own time and assimilates its ideas better than they can ; and, with the engaging confidence and inexperience of youth, he is quite certain that his ideas are far superior to any that they can have entertained. So each age judges its predecessor with a confidence and conceit all its own. It stands on its predecessor's shoulders, and because for that very reason it sees further into the future it gaily assumes that it is better fitted to understand and interpret the past. For it that particular past has not " orbed into the perfect star, We saw not when we moved therein "—if a quotation from a Victorian poet may be tolerated— because it never moved in that past at all, and perhaps the time has not yet come for any of us to see it steadily and see it whole.

When men thus speak of the Victorian age, they do not generally mean the whole of QueenVictoria's long reign of some sixty-four years from 1837 to 1901. We shall probably get at its spirit best by considering the characteristics of its middle period—that is, approximately the third quarter of the nineteeenth century, or to extend it more nearly to the length of a generation, we will say from the death of Sir Robert Peel in 1850 to the death of Lord Beaconsfield in 1881. By 1850 the spirit of the Victorian age had had time to find and express itself, and by 1881 we were verging towards the *fin de siècle* and eagerly scanning new and alluring horizons. We are now another generation ahead of 1881, we have left behind us the end of one century and are looking far forward into the next, so that if we compare the later generation with its predecessor we get a perspective sufficiently long to sustain and point the contrast.

Is the comparison altogether to the advantage of the age in which we now live ? Perhaps only a very young man would affirm with confidence that it is. His elders who have known both ages would be far less inclined to dogmatise on the point. They are not likely to discern among the teachers, thinkers, and writers of to-day many men and women of the calibre of those whom they venerated in their youth in the age when Carlyle, Macaulay, Froude, Tennyson, Browning, Dickens, Thackeray, Charlotte Brontë, George Eliot, Darwin, Herbert Spencer, Huxley, Ruskin, Matthew Arnold, and many another were still living and deeply influencing the life and thought of their time.

We do not, perhaps, rate any of these names quite so highly as their contemporaries did. We have other ideals, other standards, other problems to solve. Tennyson and Browning may neither of them have solved the riddle of the painful earth in any final sense. But they are no worse off in that respect than the greatest of their predecessors are or than the greatest of their successors are likely to be. Each generation must needs face its own obstinate questionings for itself and answer them as best it can, knowing full well that both questions and answers will differ from generation to generation. But if the character of an

99

age can be determined from the number of great names that have illustrated it and the record of great achievements it can show, surely the Victorian age need fear no comparison with that which has succeeded it.

There is, of course, another and less attractive side to the picture. The psychological atmosphere, the social fabric, the common life of the Victorian age did not immediately respond to the great intellectual influences we have enumerated. They were the still surviving products of earlier antecedents ; and those earlier antecedents did not make for expansion of thought and outlook. This side of the picture in its more homely aspects is to be found in fiction like that of Anthony Trollope, with its narrow range of sentiment, emotion, and passion, and its kindly but rather commonplace domesticities. Thus we have the somewhat paradoxical phenomenon, in the mid-Victorian age, of Trollopism, if we may so call it, existing side by side with intellectual and moral forces so disruptive as those of Darwinism and the whole theory of evolution, and apparently unaffected by them for a time. But in the next generation the new wine began to work in the old bottles, and in many departments of human life the effect has been explosive enough. An epoch of expansion has followed an epoch of concentration ; men now question everything which their fathers took contentedly and all too complacently for granted. We are nowadays nothing if not critical ; and we shall be fortunate indeed if the new age can produce for our guidance spirits as great and lofty as those of the Mid-Victorian time.

THE EFFICIENT MANNER

THE device of protective mimicry is not employed only by animals. There are many human beings who live by means of it just as much as the fly that pretends to be a wasp, and often they are hardly more aware of their own cunning than the fly of his. By some instinct of self-preservation, which works much more skilfully than any conscious design could, they acquire the outward symptoms of those mental qualities which are most wanting in them and which, therefore, they most desire to possess.

No doubt the harmless fly would give anything to possess the sting of the wasp. He cannot do that, but he has succeeded through ages of persevering effort in looking enough like a wasp to deceive some creature whom it is his interest to deceive. Man, being a superior animal, does not need such long perseverance. He can choose his own model and mimic him on his own account, and without the help of his ancestors. Indeed, in his choice of a model he follows the fashion of the day, which may change almost as quickly as fashions in dress. A generation ago, for instance, the harmless incompetent in this country often made his living by adopting an air of extreme pomposity. He spoke and behaved as if he had some important and mysterious business in hand, or as if every opinion which he expressed was the result of long thought and experience. He showed a diplomatic reserve in discussing the most trifling matters, seeming to fear that any unguarded word of his might be reported, with consequences that no one could foretell. Indeed, he conducted himself always as if in his position he owed a duty to the public, and all the while he had no position, no particular business in hand, and no opinions of his own about anything. This manner still persists in some elderly persons; but that is only because they have not enough flexibility to break themselves of it. It is no longer of any use to them, for it deceives no one. We do not now associate it with real importance, for our important people have given it up, perhaps because it has been too grossly parodied.

Its place has been taken by an efficient manner which the harmless incompetent, if he is young enough, adopts with wonderful ease. About this manner there is nothing pompous or mysterious. It is brisk, off-hand, and even confidential. It seems to display knowledge by accident and as if the displayer of it had so much that he set no store by it. He is above all things a man of the world, used to dealing with all kinds of people and able to tell them just what they want and to set them right on every point without hurting their feelings. He is, of course, deeply immersed in affairs; but he carries the burden of them lightly, usually smoking a cigarette as he talks of them, and talking as if he did everything so easily that he has plenty of time for the instruction and amusement of everybody. In expressing an opinion he often starts with the words " of course," and with a careless gesture, as if he knew that he were speaking to a man of the world who must understand. His conversation, even about matters of business, is full of gentlemanly slang and of allusions to light topics in which every gentleman is interested. But he knows when to be serious and even when to display sensibility, lowering his voice aptly to express the change of mood. In fact, he seems to be an excellent actor, unless he happens to be one by profession. For it is the mysterious curse of his incompetence that he is generally, but not particularly, efficient. Give him some piece of real business to do, and it is as if you asked the wasp-like fly to sting. He can go on behaving efficiently with perfect ease so long as he is not required to do anything. If he is, he loses his efficient manner in a moment, and becomes hurried and confused and pathetically impotent.

The worst of him is that he has never learnt to make the most of whatever small natural faculties he possesses, for they have all been absorbed in the task of protective mimicry. He has taken so much pains to appear efficient that he can no more be efficient than the wasp-like fly can be a wasp. The business of his life is not action but evasion, and that careless offhand manner of his, like the mysterious reserve of the older incompetent, is really a method of evading difficulties. Every teacher of drawing knows that the least promising student is the one who starts with a plausible imitative facility, for that very facility proves that he is not aware of the difficulties of his art. He is by nature an artistic parasite, whose one aim is to affect the symptoms of mastery without possessing it. If there had been no great artists before him he could not draw a line, for whatever he draws is in their manner or in the manner of some imitator of them, and nothing that he sets down is the result of his own experience of reality. So it is with the incompetent who acquires an efficient manner. He cannot attain to real efficiency, because he is incapable of any experience of reality. But for the example of efficient men he would be helpless in the world ; for it is they who supply him with his manner, often at second-hand, and with all the phrases and gestures which he employs as a means, not of accomplishing anything, but of evading everything.

And as the drawing of a facile student is not good to live with, so he is not good to employ. His misfortune is that he is much better at getting places than at keeping them. His manner seems impressive to those who are not used to it, so long as he is only talking about what he can do, but it raises expectations which are all the more sharply disappointed when he is required to do something. Then, too often, he is condemned as an impostor ; but the word is too harsh for him. He seldom means to deceive, for, like the facile student, he himself mistakes the symptom of mastery for the reality. He has the keenest desire to be efficient, but unfortunately he does not associate efficiency with action. It means to him merely that manner which he takes so much pains to acquire ; and he never can understand why he does not succeed like all the other efficient men. In fact, he is not made for this world, which, in spite of all its make-believe, has a constant, if obscure, relation with reality ; and we can only hope that, if he is good, he will go, when he dies, to some fitting paradise where seeming will be just the same as being.

GRUMBLING

GRUMBLING, it was lately said, is a safety-valve which the polite Frenchman denies to himself, with the result that, if he is annoyed beyond a certain point, his temper explodes like an overstrained boiler. The French Revolution itself was an explosion of that kind. The French people had endured too long and too patiently. They had nursed their grievances in silence, or aired them only in polite epigrams ; and so, when politeness gave way, the only alternative was ferocity. The moral is that we should not impose upon ourselves burdens greater than we can bear, or aim at an impossible standard of perfection.

This applies just as much to domestic as to political matters. Perfect politeness in the home is delightful and most desirable if it accurately expresses the feelings. It becomes dangerous when it ceases to express them, for then it is often a sign of mere indifference or cold contempt or of a desire to be technically in the right at all costs. As a nation we are certainly quarrelsome in our homes ; we lack the discipline of the French, to whom an open domestic quarrel is usually a very serious matter, since it expresses an exasperation long suppressed. We do not suppress our exasperations, and in consequence the domestic nuisance is rather a common object in our homes. But, on the other hand, we at least attempt much more intimacy in our homes than most other nations ; and we find that intimacy is not compatible with extreme politeness. You cannot live on the closest terms with anyone unless you tell them plainly when they irritate you in great or in small matters. If you do not tell them, their irritating habits will continue and may produce a real estrangement. There must always be some friction even between the most affectionate husbands and wives or brothers and sisters, and the way to make it harmless is to acknowledge it. It is a result of the imperfection of human nature ; and the happiness of a home is most secure when it is taken for granted that every member of it is imperfect, and when there is just as much licence allowed to imperfect patience as to other kinds of imperfection.

Just as much and no more ; for the happiness of the home, as of the State, is based upon justice. That alone makes resentments momentary and grumbling harmless. If one member of the family speaks plainly about the failings of the rest, he must allow the same plain speaking of himself. The domestic nuisance can hardly exist except where he is allowed a special privilege of grumbling, where, so far as he is concerned, it is all give and no take. The rest of the family endure him, perhaps, but their patience only teaches them to hate him. They get a habit of mute endurance, which is not a virtue if they resent silently what they endure. For this silent resentment means the total failure of domestic life, and it is not even fair to the object of it. He, from being never told of his shortcomings, indulges them more and more, until they become serious vices and make him unfit for human society. If he were opposed from the first, and provoked in others the same temper which he permitted to himself, his home would be stormier, no doubt, but it would be less unhappy. An open conflict is undignified and disagreeable ; but it soon comes to an end. Silent resentments may last for ever or break out at last in a quarrel after which there can be no reconciliation. Justice is a social virtue which, both in the State and in the family, we only learn by teaching it to each other. It cannot exist unless we exact it as well as give it. It is less spontaneous than love, and less beautiful ; but without it love has no security.

Our national weakness for grumbling is clearly connected with our national sense of justice. We grumble because there is an understanding among us that everyone has at least a right to be heard, and also that one grumbler must tolerate another. Parliament is full of grumblings in the form of questions ; but the rules which govern these all amount to this, that a member may grumble but must not nag. He must air his grievance and have done with it, and then give way to another grumbler. In fact, we have subjected our grumbling to a kind of discipline which is necessary just because we acknowledge everyone's right to grumble.

And public opinion exercises the same kind of discipline out of Parliament ; as, for instance, on a railway journey. Then, too, we acknowledge everyone's right to a short grumble ; but if the grumbler persists he loses caste among his fellow-travellers. When a French traveller begins to grumble, it is an event ; and everyone listens to him, knowing that he must have been provoked beyond all endurance and will probably make a scene. They listen with a curious silent approval of all rebellion against authority ; for they assume that he would not grumble at all without some intolerable grievance.

It is the absence of grumbling that makes authority unpopular in France and other countries ; for it is only when everyone openly grumbles at officials that they are felt to be human, and that allowances are made for their human imperfections. In England the official is a man, not an abstraction ; and when he gives himself the airs of office, we blame him and not the State. But in France he represents the State, and to quarrel with him is almost an act of insurrection. So there is little normal friction in France between the public and officials, as in the family. In England there is a good deal in both cases, but there is also, perhaps, more good will. Our habit of grumbling is undignified and wasteful, but it sometimes saves us from sudden and irreparable catastrophes, both public and private.

Modern Essays

THE FUTURE OF KNOWLEDGE

A PHILOSOPHER once said that the growth of knowledge in the last ninety years had been so great that we
could not realise it, for it had revolutionised our whole
view of the world; and he wondered what would be
the position of our remote descendants if knowledge
continued to increase at the same rate for another
500 years. It is not clear whether he was thinking of
their material position or of their state of mind: but
most people nowadays, when they speculate about
the future, concern themselves with the former rather
than with the latter. They do not understand that
our vast increase of knowledge is itself the result of a
state of mind which desires knowledge above all things,
and that knowledge will increase only so long as that
state of mind continues. We are so used to it now
that we assume it to be normal in civilised societies.
Indeed we can scarcely conceive a civilisation without
it. Yet, among all the great societies of the past,
only the Greeks at the height of their energy were
consumed by a passion for knowledge, and even in
their minds it had several rivals, while in modern
Europe it began to gain predominance at the Renaissance, and did not become supreme until the nineteenth
century.

Other societies, of course, have desired and acquired
knowledge, but none has even organised itself so completely as ours for this particular purpose, or absorbed

its greatest energies, its best talents, and its noblest enthusiasm in this particular cause. Leonardo da Vinci, whom we think of as the typical man of the Renaissance, was in his life prophetic of the future course of the modern world. Unlike any former artist known to us, he, though capable of the greatest things in art, gave himself up more and more to the pursuit of knowledge, which he desired for its own sake and to satisfy his boundless curiosity about the nature of things. What happened to him has since happened to the common mind of Europe. The best part of it has been drawn more and more into the same pursuit, and now we are lost in wonder at its triumphs.

But these triumphs will continue only so long as they satisfy the finest and most disinterested minds. We cannot assume that the appetite for knowledge will always grow with what it feeds on. It will persist only so long as it contents the spirit of man, and there are signs already of a revolt against its supremacy. To this revolt knowledge itself contributes, for our eager curiosity about the past has made us less complacent about the present. The more we learn about the life and the mind of past societies, the more we become aware that in some respects the men of these societies have surpassed us in the art of living. We may smile at their blind speculations about the nature of the material world, but we are often surprised at the profound wisdom of their sayings about the mind of man ; and slowly we realise that our own energies are limited like theirs, and that, if we give them all to the pursuit of knowledge of things outside us, we cannot excel either in the knowledge of ourselves or in the exercise of those faculties that are not purely intellectual.

It is commonly supposed that the more we know of the material world, the more we must know about everything; but that belief is not confirmed by experience. Our knowledge of the material world, for instance, has supplied us with many theories about the relation of man to the universe; but none of these has yet been of much use to us in the art of living. We are wonderfully fertile in ideas, but we have very little power of applying them. Indeed, we are for the most part content to talk about them, and so they have their vogue and grow stale almost as quickly as fashions of dress. They satisfy by their rapid changes the surface curiosity of our minds; but all the while our deeper and finer desires remain unsatisfied, for we form no constant ideal of life that will satisfy them. We have fanatics in the pursuit of knowledge, like Browning's grammarian; but, though we may admire them, we cannot make them our pattern. They seem to us, for all their disinterestedness, to have forgotten the means in the end. They are altogether specialists; and the mind of man cannot content itself with any kind of specialism.

That is a simple fact that we are beginning to learn; and the more we become aware of it, the less likely we are to rest content with the highly organised specialism of our modern society. The ideal of that specialism is a society that shall resemble a hive of bees, each individual blindly absorbed in his task and losing all his individuality in the performance of it. As the

bees make honey, so shall men make knowledge ; and
it is assumed that the generations of men will be as
subservient to this passion for knowledge as generations
of bees are to their common instinct for work. But
men are not, and never have been, specialised like
bees. They look before and after, and pine for what
is not ; and the more their desires are satisfied in one
direction, the stronger they become in another. We
have attained to a stability of knowledge without any
precedent ; but it only makes us the more aware of our
extraordinary instability of faith, and of ideas based
upon faith. It is not merely that we are sceptical
about theological dogmas ; we suffer from a much
more profound and more unwilling scepticism about
the proper aims of life, and no advances in material
knowledge satisfy the questions raised by this scepticism.

We have our morals, of course ; but, so far as these
are systematic, it is only a working system not based
upon any conception of the universe. We have also
our emotions, but we are apt to regard these as mere
survivals. We are afraid of them all, and have almost
given up the attempt to train them by means of art or
of a beautiful way of living. In fact, we starve all
our faculties except those that are purely intellectual.
Yet those faculties remain, and are arousing in us an
increasing desire for their exercise. If this desire
continues to grow, it will sooner or later divert our
higher energies from the pursuit of knowledge to
other ends. We shall be more concerned with being
than with knowing, and our whole civilisation will

change its nature in a new Renaissance. That will mean, perhaps, a great loss, but it will also mean a great gain, if it gives us a life more harmonious and more clear of purpose.

PLEASURE AND COMFORT

ANYONE who reads Pepys's Diary with the object of discovering in what respect the life of his time differed most sharply from the life of ours must notice at once that he enjoyed far more pleasures than any man of his class could enjoy now. We know, of course, that he loved pleasure inordinately ; but that also is a point of difference. No one now loves pleasure as he loved it—at least no one would take so much pains to seek it. Those who are supposed to lead a life of pleasure nowadays expect it to come to them. They sit and wait for it, and it seldom comes. But Pepys pursued it as a child runs after a butterfly, and wherever he went he found it. We are not speaking now of forbidden pleasures, which left even him weary and sated, but of innocent delights which never tired him and which he wrote down in his Diary so that he might be reminded of them in the future. We may be repelled by him sometimes, but at other times we cannot help loving and envying him simply for his power of enjoying the pleasures that sprang up about him wherever he went. And we envy him not only for his temperament, but also for his opportunities. There

were so many other people ready to sing or dance with
him. It was so easy then to start a frolic; and it
still remained easy when Dr. Johnson could be drawn
into one in the middle of the night. Even he, for all
his melancholy and solitary labours, led far more of a
life of pleasure than most young sparks of to-day.
He, too, knew how to enjoy himself, and found everywhere pleasures to be enjoyed.

But, if we regret the easy pleasures of the past,
there is one consolation that is sure to be offered to
us. We may not live in an age of pleasure, we are
told, but we do live in an age of comfort, and we should
not be able to endure the discomforts which were so
much a matter of course to Pepys that he seldom even
mentions them. That is true enough. Perhaps the
greatest change which distinguishes the present from
the past is the substitution of comfort for pleasure.
There is no reason that we can see why we should not
have the pleasure of the past as well as our own comfort; but the fact remains that we have given up the
one for the other.

Those " serious " people who were so predominant
in the second quarter of the nineteenth century condemned many harmless pleasures for their worldliness,
but they do not seem to have raised any such objec-
tion against comforts. Indeed, they made a life of
comfort seem respectable to everyone, and taught us
that it was a breach of the Sabbath to dance, but not
to spend the afternoon sleeping in a soft armchair.
Under their patronage comfort became a thoroughly
God-fearing word, while at the same time pleasure got

an unlawful sound. They would talk of home comforts
readily enough, but not of home pleasures ; and they
had good reason, for their well-ordered homes did
indeed contain a great many comforts but very few
pleasures. They might be enervating, but at least
they were not delightful ; and they were distinguished
by their expensive decorum from the cheerful and less
comfortable homes of the poor.

It is curious that comfort should ever have appeared
less worldly than pleasure, for comfort of all things is
most easily bought with money. Anyone who can
afford it can buy a first-class ticket for the journey of
life ; but, however much you pay for pleasure, you
cannot make sure of enjoying it. We, however, have
come to believe that pleasure can be bought like
comfort ; with the result that we get very little of it,
though we have lost our fathers' suspicion of it.

The reason is that we want to be comfortable in all
our pleasures. We do not understand that, while
comfort is passive and negative, pleasure is active
and adventurous. The armchair is the type of the
one and the dance of the other, and they cannot be
combined in one delight. In our effort to combine
them we may hire wonderful dancers, or singers, or
players to entertain us ; but we are still far from the
pleasure of Pepys, who knew how to entertain himself, and so was master of delights that could not be
bought with money. He would go out adventurously
in search of pleasure, and make it wherever he went.
He would pipe so that others might dance, and dance
to any one's piping. He was never in a hurry to get

from one place to another, but took whatever he could find by the way, and he was justly proud of his power of enjoyment. He tried to write a song in praise of a liberal genius, such as he conceived his own to be. There he was right, for he had indeed a liberal genius for pleasure, and took pains to cultivate it.

That is where we fail; in our confusion of pleasure with comfort we associate it with idleness. We speak of an idle, pleasure-loving fellow as if the two went naturally together. But an idle man can scarcely know enough of real pleasure to love it. Even if he pursue it in a motor-car, it will always escape him. Pepys was as industrious in work as in play. He was President of the Royal Society as well as a high and trusted official; and we may be sure that his active pleasures increased his power of work. But the typical pleasure-lover of our time expects everything to be done for him. It is an old joke that he makes a pretence of enjoying nothing; but there is less pretence in that than we suppose. He is weary, indeed, not of pleasure itself, but of waiting for it at his ease, for he always waits in vain.

"THE LAW OF PROGRESS"

The Dean of St. Paul's, in a lecture upon the Spirit of the Age, remarked that we must discount very seriously some of the hopes that have been built upon the supposed law of progress. But there are many people now who, if those hopes were denied to them, would have none at all, and the present weakening of the belief in a continuous improvement of the state of man in this life is beginning to cause much confusion and distress in men's minds. An immense hope has traversed the world, and, if now it seems delusive, it is likely to be followed by a despair no less immense. The modern world, as a whole, has committed itself to this belief in a continuous improvement; for a century or more men's hearts and minds have been fed upon it; upon that they have founded their faith in the ultimate righteousness of the universe, and if it crumbles away, what grounds of faith will be left to them ?

It has been said that if Aristotle could have known the history of Europe for a thousand years after his death, his heart would have been broken; yet he lived when the boundless hopes of the great age of Greece had already been falsified. What would the men of the generation after Marathon have said if they could have foreseen the future of their country ? They were fed upon hopes greater than any which the modern world has known—hopes of which the ruined monument still shines upon the Acropolis and the broken music still sounds in our ears. Yet even in their lifetime that decline began which was to turn the Hellene into the " Graeculus esuriens," half pitied, half despised by the satirist of a conquering race.

It was not merely that the sceptre passed away from Greece. That might have been a righteous punishment of the Greeks themselves; but, worse than that,

Modern Essays

the moral ideas of the great age were wasted like water
spilt in the desert. For centuries no society was governed by exalted hopes or aims ; the individual was
left to find what faith he could out of his own private
experience of life ; and the change is expressed with
melancholy grandeur in the words of one who ruled
the world and yet despaired of it :—" The poet hath
said, Dear city of Cecrops ; and shall I not say, Dear
city of God ? "

The chief interest for us in the meditations of Marcus
Aurelius is that they express the faith of a man for
whom hope of all kinds had been reduced to a mini-
mum. It may be that in a few generations our descendants will have to undergo the ordeal through
which he passed. It is true that they will know more
about the material facts of life than he knew, but we
cannot be sure that their greater knowledge will give
them greater hope. It seems to us now that science
has given to civilisation a power which nothing can
destroy ; but what if it uses that power to destroy
itself, if our society is mastered by its machinery and
men come to feel themselves mere individuals at the
mercy of blind material forces, with no help except
what their own souls give to them ?

At present we nearly all have a comfortable sense
of the purpose and power of society. It means to us
more than a number of private persons, each living as
best he can ; we think of European civilisation as a
single force making for righteousness, as something
stronger than all the follies and crimes of individuals,
or even of statesmen.

But this sense of collective power and righteousness
has been shared by very few ages or nations in the
history of the world. Men for the most part have
lived their lives unfortified by it ; and often govern-
ment has seemed to them merely the chief expression
in the world of that evil which all religions and philosophies have tried to account for without teaching
despair. Faith in progress has been for many of us a
substitute for these religions and philosophies ; and
to the mystics and eremites of the East our ideas of
life must seem like the ideas of the children of the rich,
for whom the world is a warm nursery and cold and
hunger merely themes for pretty stories. Our theories,
they would say, are the result of our own good fortune ;
disaster would scatter them all and leave us naked to
the cold blasts of reality.

Yet the very loss of faith in progress has its own
consolation. Those who have that faith believe that
progress means happiness, and look for happiness there.
When the faith declines, men do not necessarily despair
of happiness, but look for it elsewhere ; and the loss
of faith in progress does not imply the end of all
effort to improve the life of men, or a spiritless acquiescence in every kind of oppression. Whether we
believe in progress or not, the idea of duty remains,
and it is not strengthened, but may be weakened, by
a belief in progress. Mechanical optimism tempts
men to shift their responsibilities on to something not
themselves that makes for righteousness. We have
seen that very clearly in the economic optimism of
the nineteenth century, in the curious belief that

money-making must be a benefit to the community, however it is made, and that for those who make it duty and interest are miraculously and certainly identified. That belief at any rate was founded on an illusion, on a deliberate blindness to the force of evil which persists through all human effort and which threatens to pervert it at every turn. Evil is a fact which no belief in progress dan destroy, and which is only strengthened when a mechanical optimism tries to conceal it.

And the strange thing is that men get more happiness and a surer faith from facing it than from ignoring it. Just as in art a great tragedy, like *King Lear*, leaves us with a stronger belief in righteousness than any cheerful tale with a conventionally happy ending, so in life itself there is a half-conscious insecurity in all our hopes so long as we are ignorant or regardless of the evil of life. We know in our hearts then that our palace of hope is built on the sand; and men have often turned to the extreme of pessimism merely from disgust of such insecurity. Indeed, all the pessimism of philosophy and all the fierce logic of Calvinism are the result of a desire to find the rock of ultimate reality, and to build what can be built on that. Faiths dependent on passing circumstance and the sudden successes of a fortunate age will never satisfy the mind of man for long. He must know the worst before he can honestly hope for the best; and his knowledge must be based upon the experience of all mankind, in times of material despair as in times of material confidence, if he is to put any lasting trust in it.

Modern Essays

LIVING IN THE PAST

COULD a man, were he given the opportunity, really live in any age widely remote from his own ? Modern philosophy tells us that life is then at its highest and best when the organism is perfectly adapted to its environment. If this be so, then it is clear that any large, sudden, and abrupt change in the environment must impair the vitality of the organism and might even destroy it altogether. If we think of it, a Greek of the age of Pericles, a Roman of the age of Julius Cæsar, would find it as hard to live the life of to-day as any man now alive would find it hard to live on were he by some freak of magic to fall asleep in his own world to-night and to wake up to-morrow morning in the Athens of Pericles or in the Rome of Julius Cæsar. The mere effort of the organism to adapt itself to the strange environment would benumb all its energies and arrest all its functions. You might as well expect a palm tree to flourish in the Arctic regions. It would languish and die in the attempt.

Yet there are many worthy people, who delight to call themselves old-fashioned, and are always longing, so they pretend, to live in some other and better age than their own. They make to themselves a Paradise of a past they have never known, and fondly imagine that were they its Adam and Eve no serpent would ever beguile them in wanting to know the good and the evil of the present. It is a vain aspiration, and

those who entertain it only succeed, so far as they
succeed at all, in getting hopelessly out of touch with
their own age. That may or may not be a good thing
in itself, but it is certainly a very different thing from
living in any other age. We have no other age than
our own to live in; and the true wisdom of life is frankly
to live in our own age and to make the best of it,
neither bewailing the past, of which, having no personal experience, we make to ourselves an ideal necessarily more or less false, nor disparaging the present
merely because it is no easy thing to live well and make
the best of life in any age.

Hans Andersen seems to us to have fathomed the
philosophy of the subject in his own inimitable fashion
in one of his enchanting tales, " The Overshoes of
Fortune." A large company was gathered together
at an evening party at a house in Copenhagen. The
entertainment was at its height, and " the conversation turned upon the Middle Ages. Some considered
that period much more interesting than our own time :
Yes, Councillor Knap defended this view so zealously
that the lady of the house went over at once to his side.
. . . The Councillor considered the times of the Danish
King Hans as the noblest and happiest age." Now
while this discussion was going on in the drawing-
room two fairies had made their way into the hall.
One was the handmaid of Fortune, who called herself
Happiness, and was entrusted with the distribution
of Fortune's more trifling gifts. The older and elder
was Care herself, who knew better than to trust anyone but herself to do such a business as hers. The

maid of Fortune had a pair of overshoes, which it was her mission to bring to the human race. "These overshoes," she explained to Care, "have the property that everyone who puts them on is at once transported to the time and place in which he likes to be—every wish in reference to time, place, and circumstance is at once fulfilled ; and so for once man can be happy here below ! " " Believe me," said Care, " he will be very unhappy, and will bless the moment when he can get rid of the overshoes again." The overshoes were left in the hall, and Councillor Knap on his departure put them on, mistaking them for his own. Still full of his desire to live in the times of King Hans, he found himself transported to those times the moment he left the house. After a few adventures and experiences quite natural in the circumstances, but exceedingly disconcerting to the luckless *laudator temporis acti*, he managed to get rid of the overshoes, and straightway found himself back in his own familiar life. " He thought of the terror and anxiety he had undergone, and praised from his heart the happy present, our own time, which, with all its shortcomings, was far better than the period in which he had been placed a short time before." After this the overshoes got into other hands—or rather, on to other feet—and played many a shrewd and frolicsome prank with those who successively wore them. But in every case each one who wore them was heartily glad to be rid of them.

The gifts of Fortune, Andersen would teach us, are, after all, unkind. Eagerly as you may yearn for them, you will find when they come that they bring with them, not the better and happier life you asked for, but care, trouble, bewilderment, and disappointment. You may think that your life is " cabin'd, cribb'd, confined " by time, place, and circumstance. The overshoes of Fortune will, indeed, emancipate you from what you call this thraldom, but only to teach you that it is better to bear those ills you have than fly to others that you know not of.

Such is the plain moral of the very pretty tale. But a deeper moral is to follow. At last the overshoes are worn by one who realises that it is neither time, place, nor circumstance that makes for true happiness. " In my own heart," he exclaims, " I know very well what I want; I want to attain the happy goal, the happiest of all." Straightway he finds himself in his own coffin, to all appearance dead. The effort to change his environment, to seek a happiness not to be found in any external change of time, place, or circumstance, has extinguished his personality altogether. The two fairies reappear. Care asks what happiness the overshoes have brought to men. " They have at least brought a permanent happiness to him who slumbers here," replies the handmaid of Fortune. " Oh, no ! " says Care. " He went away of himself; he was not summoned. His spirit was not strong enough to lift the treasures he had been destined to lift. I will do him a favour." She drew the overshoes from his feet, and the man awoke from his sleep—even from the sleep of death. Let us hope that he lived thenceforth a wiser, a better, and a more contented man. Anyhow, " Care vanished, and with her the

Modern Essays

overshoes disappeared too ; doubtless she looked upon them as her own property."

There have been many moralisings since the world began on " the vanity of human wishes," but perhaps this of Hans Andersen's is one of the wisest and tenderest of them all. Other and sterner moralists have rebuked the unruly ambitions of men. Hans Andersen chides their less unlovely reactions with a gentleness all his own. To desire to live in some golden age of the past is a very graceful form of reaction, and in the pages of Ruskin and Carlyle it was certainly made to look a very attractive one. But in truth it is an idle dream. There is no golden age of the past—in spite of Carlyle and all that he wrote in *Past and Present*, in spite of Ruskin and all that he wrote in many a glowing page. The only golden age that mankind will ever know is that which they make for themselves out of the time and place and circumstances which environ their own fleeting existence. It is, as we have said, no easy thing to live well and make the best of life in any age. The overshoes of Fortune will not help us in the least. They belong to Care, not to Happiness.

MUTUAL ADMIRATION SOCIETIES

THERE is something peculiarly irritating in mutual admiration societies, to those who are outside them, just as there is often something irritating in the in-

125

fatuation of lovers. But we bear with lovers because
we all have been, or are, or may be in love ; whereas
most of us at least pretend that we would scorn to
belong to a mutual admiration society. We would
rather be like the miller who cared for nobody and
nobody cared for him. He was jolly because he had
no illusions, whereas mutual admiration societies
seldom seem jolly to outsiders and thrive upon illusions.
It is the illusions that irritate us ; we long to dispel
them, to tell A that B is not a genius, but rather below
the average both in wits and in looks. And we are
sure that A would not believe us, only because he
barters admiration with B and will not get it unless
he gives it. That is where we make the mistake, for
the theory of the Social Contract will no more apply
to mutual admiration societies than to society at
large. They also are not made, but grow. They
may be based upon illusion ; but, if they are, it follows
that the illusion must be honest, for no one, however
hungry of admiration, could enjoy it if he knew it
was unreal. It is in this respect, being mutual, utterly
different from flattery. For flattery, however gross
or insincere, is always a tribute to our importance.
Though we know that the flatterer does not mean what
he says, still he would not flatter us at all if we were
not worth flattery ; and by doing so he confesses his
own inferiority. But the members of a mutual
admiration society are on equal terms. They give
and take, not flattery, but admiration ; and that admiration, if not sincere, is of no significance whatever.
There may be some exaggeration in their expression

of it, the exaggeration that is constantly produced by the action of mind upon mind, and by a sense of general agreement in any body of men ; but exaggeration is an utterly different thing from pure fiction, being usually unconscious in all its stages.

The fact is, there is usually something ignoble in our irritation at mutual admiration societies, and in our itch to dispel their illusions ; something of the ugly impulse that set Iago plotting against Othello and Desdemona. We are envious of a little world within the world, whose inhabitants seem to have some faith, some secret of power, denied to the rest of us. For there can be no doubt that mutual admiration societies have a secret of power, and that the members of them often accomplish what they could never have done alone. When they do great things they are no longer accused of mutual admiration, as treason, when it prospers, is not called treason ; for then the world admits that the mutual admiration was justified, however absurd it may have seemed beforehand.

But mutual admiration societies are justified, not merely by the quality of their members, but by the effect they often have upon members who alone would have done nothing. Take the case of the Pre-Raphaelites, not merely the brotherhood, but all of those who came under the influence of Rossetti. How many of them were raised above their natural powers by the association with him and with each other, which certainly was based upon a very strong system of mutual admiration ? To Rossetti geese of the right kind were always swans ; and often they turned into swans for a time at his bidding. So and so, he would say, was a " stunner," and must be an artist ; and the wonder was that so and so did often become an artist of some merit, to fall back into mediocrity as soon as he fell out of that society. They all, at any rate, had the benefit of a clear direction. Rossetti told them that art was the only thing worth having in life, and he also told them how to set about producing it. They found salvation of a kind with Rossetti for their prophet, and their lives were heightened by finding it.

But from the first even the most mediocre of them were redeemed from complete mediocrity by the fact that they could recognise a prophet in Rossetti, and could submit themselves to him ; and this common fact was no doubt the real basis of their mutual admiration. It was what distinguished them all from the rest of the world ; and there is the same kind of distinction in the members of all mutual admiration societies. To others they will often seem a set of absurd persons making a fuss about nothing. To themselves there must appear to be virtue in each one of them, because he has seen that it is worth while to belong to their brotherhood, although there is no money to be made out of it. For mutual admiration societies are always disinterested in their aim, however narrow and absurd that aim may be ; and that is what makes a brotherhood of them and accounts for their mutual admiration. There is no brotherhood in a limited company; its members are distinguished by no common desire, except the desire to make money, which is no distinction. Anyone who can buy shares can be a member of it, and their association is a mere accident. It is not accident that brings together the members of a mutual admiration society, but common tastes and a common aim, of which mutual admiration is a natural result. For these common tastes and common aims do indeed reveal men to each other and discover their finer qualities; since it is by reason of their finer qualities that they are brought together. They may idealise each other, but the ideal is based upon reality; and perhaps they know more of each other, after all, than those who pride themselves on having no delusions about human nature. For it is a deadlier error to mistake swans for geese than to mistake geese for swans, since you can never turn a swan into a goose by miscalling it.

WHAT MIGHT HAVE BEEN

THERE is perhaps no more idle form of speculation in which we poor mortals can indulge than that which deals with what might have been. And yet the temptation to indulge in it is one which at times obstinately besets nearly every man who ever thinks at all, who ever " looks before and after, and pines for what is not." The inexorable issues of cause and effect often seem at the outset of a great train of historic events to be poised on so delicate a knife-edge that the lightest of material things, or even the faintest breath of what seems to be the wind of accident, might turn the

balance one way or the other. The balance turns,
and the die is cast. Thenceforth the train of events
is foreordained and ineluctable.

> " The moving finger writes ; and having writ
> Moves on : nor all your piety and wit
> Shall lure it back to cancel half a line,
> Nor all your tears wash out a word of it."

And yet we look back to the moment when the balance
was still unbiassed, and can hardly help saying to
ourselves, " If only one trivial little thing had been
different, if judgment, motive, purpose, or even what
we call accident had inclined by a hair's-breadth in
another direction, all would have been different and
the current of the world's history might have been
turned into another channel." All would have been
different, no doubt, but that is all we can safely say or
reasonably think. There is no calculus subtle enough
to enable us even to guess what might have been if,
let us say, Chatham's mental eclipse had occurred in
the midst of the Seven Years War, or had not occurred
when the issues of peace and war between England
and the American Colonies were hanging in the balance ;
or if Napoleon had died in infancy ; or if Bismarck
had not so edited the famous Ems despatch as to
render it provocative enough for his purpose ; or if
in the elections of 1885 Gladstone had obtained what
he asked for—namely, a majority independent of the
Irish vote.

To this little breed of men, so eager in their curiosity
and yet so puny in their penetration, speculations such

as these, however inviting they may be, are nevertheless utterly futile. We can only say with Bishop Butler, " Things are what they are, and their consequences will be what they will be." It is little, as experience is constantly teaching us, that we can forecast of the ulterior consequences—or even of many of the immediate consequences—of any great decision that has to be taken in the life of a nation or in the life of an individual. It is much less that we can even conjecture of what the consequences might have been had that decision been other than it was. Human events are not isolated in their effects. Their articulations and their reciprocal concatenations are infinite and wholly incalculable. Who could have forecast all the immeasurable effects of the seemingly trivial accident of the fall of an apple in Newton's garden ? Or again, if we consider only the life of the individual, the ulterior consequences of any hypothetical change in a man's actions as he did them are in reality equally inscrutable. Of those of us who have reached or passed middle age there must be few who have not thought to themselves at one time or another, " If I had my life to live over again how differently I should have acted at this or that conjuncture."

And yet the reflection, however spontaneous and inevitable, really involves a whole series of irreconcilable antinomies. It raises in the first place the whole question of freedom of the will. If the will is not free, clearly there was no choice open to the man at the conjuncture in which he now thinks he would act otherwise than he did. In that alternative, and on the hypothesis that the experience of his past life is still with him in the life that he is now living over again, it is hard to conceive of a more excruciating torture than for a man to live over again and have to make in succession all his old mistakes, well knowing that they are mistakes and that he has no power to correct them. That would indeed be a worse hell than even the sombre genius of Dante ever conceived.

On the other hand, if the will is free, there is no doubt a theoretical way of escape from this unspeakable Inferno. But it is a way that can only be trodden at the sacrifice of personal identity. The idea that a man could correct his former mistakes, if he had to live his life over again, is totally devoid of content and has in truth no intelligible meaning unless we assume that his personal identity and his consciousness of personal identity remain unchanged and unimpaired throughout the process. If in living his life over again he is to lose all memory and all consciousness of his former life, then for all practical purposes he is not the same man but another man altogether, and there seems to be no reason whatever why that other man should avoid any of the mistakes that the original man formerly committed. If, on the other hand, he retains his personal identity and says to himself in consequence, "Here and here in my former life I made this or that mistake, and this is what I am now going to avoid," then again it follows that his personality will and must be changed in the process, and may be changed to such an extent that his

Modern Essays

personal identity will in course of time disappear. He will become another man, and by the time that other man has reached the age at which the original man made the reflection on which we are commenting there will be no identity, and perhaps even no resemblance, between their respective experiences.

This is not, of course, to say that a man's personality is exclusively the product of his experiences. But it is certainly not independent of them. There is an initial, native, and individual element in personality which comes from we know not where, and consists in we know not what. But this primordial element is gradually overlaid and developed by the experiences, the actions, and the decisions of life—each leaving its impress and deposit on the personality, until in the end the only connecting link between the original and acquired personality appears to be the abiding consciousness of personal identity. If that be lost or obliterated in the process, there is no longer the same man, but another; and the experience of the one is no longer of any use either to admonish, to guide, or to correct the actions of the other. The truth is that the whole speculation is an idle and, indeed, an impossible one. We cannot separate experience from personality after the fashion it implies. If the one is changed, the other is changed with it, and nothing in either can thenceforth be exactly as it was before. Tennyson taught us that we cannot even isolate a flower from its surroundings and flatter ourselves that we know all or even much about it; much less can we

133

do the same by the problems of history and the
mysteries of personality :—

> " Flower in the crannied wall,
>   I pluck you out of the crannies—
>   Hold you here, root and all, in my hand,
>   Little flower—but if I could understand
>   What you are, root and all, and all in all
>   I should know what God and man is."

THE PERSPECTIVE OF LIFE

In an early scene of M. Rostand's famous play of
Chantecler there is a passage which points very pertin-
ently to an exceedingly common trait of human nature.
Speaking of the eponymous hero of the play, the
Turkey, a personage of great importance and of even
greater self-importance, remarks :

> " Je l'ai vu naître.
> Ce poussin—car pour moi c'est toujours un poussin—
> Venait prendre chez moi sa leçon de buccin."

Elderly people, especially if they are commonplace and
self-important, are very prone to this distortion of
perspective in their judgment of men younger than
themselves, especially if the latter have either achieved
greatness or had greatness thrust on them. In the
particular case we need not take Chantecler at his own
estimate, or even at the estimate formed of him by
the more obsequious denizens of his native farmyard,
in order to recognise that the Turkey's estimate is
fundamentally a false one. Because we have known

a man from his birth, because we are aware of his lowly
origin, because we have had a share in his education,
because we have given him early lessons in the art of
blowing his own trumpet—these are, in truth, no
good reasons why we should judge him throughout
his career, be it worthy or unworthy, from that particular and very ill-chosen point of view. Yet " pour
moi c'est toujours un poussin " is assuredly the far too
common attitude of the former tutor towards his
quondam pupil, and even in general of elderly people
towards their juniors. A man must needs adjust his
perspective of life very carefully and very dispas-
sionately if he would avoid this almost universal
error. May we not say that the party history of
the last generation might have been very different
if the attitude of the elder Tories towards that im-
portunate young Chanteceler Lord Randolph Churchill
had not so obviously been " pour moi c'est toujours un
poussin " ?

It is the same perhaps in all departments of human
activity. It is only by an effort of mental detachment
that those of an older generation can bring themselves to understand that the rising generation is going
to live its own life, that its life will differ in many
respects from their life, that its heroes will not be their
heroes, nor its ideals their ideals ; in a word, that the
chicks of to-day—whose lowly origin, it may be, and
early efforts, possibly grotesque, at self-assertion their
elders have known and scorned—are going to be the
Chanteclers of to-morrow. When they were young
they may have looked up, possibly with exaggerated

respect, to those who had already arrived, and have acknowledged, rightly or wrongly, that they were made of finer clay than themselves. Can they without an effort think the same thing of the " poussins " of to-day—"toujours poussins," as they regard them, albeit full-fledged Chanteclers to themselves and their juniors ?

Yet in any true perspective of life the " poussins " of to-day are probably just as worthy or just as unworthy of their exalted positions as the acknowledged Chanteclers of the past. It should be remembered that these, too, were " poussins " in their time, that even among their elders there were middle-aged and self-important Turkeys who had seen them hatched and had vilipended them with the self-satisfied yet wholly unconvincing phrase, " pour moi c'est toujours un poussin." It seems a mere commonplace to say that we should judge each man of eminence on his own merits and not misjudge him because we have known him in his nonage and had not the wit to foresee that he was going to be eminent. Yet this is what many of us are constantly doing.

There is no relation of life in which this petrifying attitude of " pour moi c'est toujours un poussin " is more common or more mischievous than that of parents to their children. We have all known our children as " poussins," and our tender solicitude for their youth and inexperience is very apt to lead us still to treat them as "poussins" long after their spurs and their hackles have begun to grow. To know when their children have grown up and are entitled to think and act for themselves is one of the hardest lessons that parents have to learn, so hard indeed that very many parents never do learn it. Of all the causes of estrangement between parents and their adult children none is perhaps so frequent and so fertile as this inability of parents to understand that the period of " poussinage," so to speak, must come to an end, that their children are becoming men and women like themselves, and that friendly counsel and companionship must take the place of parental authority and tutelage.

There is plenty of good advice available from the pulpit and elsewhere concerning the duty of children towards their parents. But, as the late Dr. Creighton once insisted in a memorable sermon at St. Paul's, we might with advantage hear more than we do concerning the reciprocal duty of parents towards their children. " The old," he said, " are masters of the situation. If the young break away from them the fault must be largely theirs. . . . . There is no more beautiful sight than to see young faces brighten when an old man enters the room ; to hear young lips refer to his judgment in their perplexities ; to feel that a strong bond of mutual sympathy and regard exists between them. There is no more saddening sight than to hear young voices hush before an old man's coming ; to see animated faces grow resigned ; to feel that the young heart closes as against a stranger, and that sympathy has no place."

Is not the clue to this melancholy contrast to be found in the phrase " pour moi c'est toujours un poussin " ? We cannot give the young their due, nor

can we do our own duty by them, so long as we persist
in holding, as too many parents do, that because we
have known and loved them in their cradles, because
we have long exercised just and necessary authority
over them, therefore they must always obey us and
never have wills and opinions of their own. " Do
not try," says the preacher we have quoted, " to alter
the development of a young heart ; try only to direct
it.   Remove difficulties, ward off dangers, give strength
by the knowledge that you are always ready to aid."
That is the true wisdom, and, in truth, the whole duty
of the parent whose children are no longer " poussins."

PRACTICAL JOKES

PRACTICAL jokes are still common, and it is worth
while to inquire what is the motive of them.   They
may be distinguished from the older kind of practical
joke, of which Theodore Hook was the great master,
in that their victim is the public and not some particular person.   The older kind has gone out of fashion
except among high-spirited youths, who still perhaps
set booby-traps and make apple-pie beds.   The rest of
us have become more civilised in our sense of humour ;
and, if we are to laugh at an individual, he must himself supply the reason why we should laugh at him.
To make him seem ridiculous by means of a practical
joke is to cheat ourselves into laughter.   Even if it is
not cruel, it is bad art, like the mechanical excitements

supplied by the scenery of the melodrama. But practical jokes practised on the public at large are still
popular, partly because the public, not knowing who
has practised them, cannot take its revenge, and partly
because they make a stir which gives the joker a sense
of power. He, no doubt, is usually a man who could
not produce any kind of effect upon the public mind
by any rational exercise of his faculties. To those
who know him and have to do with him in the ordinary
routine of his life he is a nobody; but, if he can set the
world talking by means of a practical joke, he seems to
himself a somebody, even though the world cannot put
a name to him. He wins only an anonymous notoriety
for a moment; but even that flatters him, for it means
that he has a secret over which he can chuckle. In
one respect at least he is wiser than all the world, for
he alone knows who has played the joke upon it.

Officials, as representing the public, are often the
victims of this kind of joke; and when it is practised
upon them it has rather more point than when it is
practised upon the public at large. For officials, besides representing the public, are commonly regarded
as misrepresenting them, and therefore as being their
enemies; and, since they have more power of revenge
than the public at large, there is more danger in hoaxing them. Thus the practical joke of the Captain of
Koepenick met with a good deal of sympathy, for the
public always like to laugh at officials; and, further,
it was a real practical joke, in that it was a practical
reduction to an absurdity of the soldier's habit of blind,
mechanical obedience. In this case the joker merely

pressed a button, as it were, which he had no right to press, with the result that men behaved as if they were machines set in motion by a purely material force. They themselves supplied a great part of the joke by their readiness to obey anyone ; and it was a joke that could not have been played on them but for that weakness. It was, in fact, a satire upon discipline, and the very simplicity of the means by which it was produced only added to the force of it.

The term practical joke would have more point if it were used only of tricks of this kind—tricks which, like the plot of a good comedy, merely give the victims a chance of making themselves ridiculous. In its broader sense it is commonly a misnomer, for it is used of tricks which, however practical, are not jokes at all, since they do not illustrate or expose any weakness in the victim.

To ring a door-bell and then run away is not a joke, because to answer the bell when it is rung is a natural and proper practice with no individual absurdity in it. If that kind of joke amuses the joker, it is only because he is pleased with any exercise of his own power. Theodore Hook once gave a list in his own magazine of practical jokes which he thought amusing, and they are nearly all of this pointless kind. One was to tie a piece of meat securely to the bell-handles which dangle outside the gates of certain suburban villas in the hope that every passing dog would grab at the meat and set the bell ringing. Probably the fun here lies in the notion that the inhabitants of suburban villas are an absurd people, whose function is to

be the victims of a harlequinade in real life. To do
Hook justice, he ends with a story illustrating the
dangers of practical joking ; but the fact remains that
he thought his practical jokes were real jokes, whereas
they were not jokes at all but mere human imitations
of the cruelties of chance. Indeed, most practical
jokers only prove their inability to make a real joke by
their inordinate desire to do so. Nothing amuses them
so much as a trick of chance played upon some one
else ; and they try to repeat this amusement by playing the part of chance themselves. M. Bergson, the
philosopher of laughter, explains their sense of humour·
but nothing can excuse it.

IDEALISM OF OUR TIME

MR. BALFOUR, presiding at a lecture given by Sir
Ernest Shackleton, said that the idealism of our time
was not inferior to that of our forefathers ; and in
proof of this he contrasted our Polar expeditions, in
which there is " no territory to be gained, no enemies
to be conquered, no vulgar ambition to be satisfied,"
with the adventures of Elizabethan voyagers, which
had always some material aim. The point is a good
one ; for, in spite of all the splendour and bravery of
the Elizabethan age, and the eloquence with which it
expressed itself, it was indeed an age of less idealism
than our own. M. Jusserand, an impartial foreigner
whose knowledge of that age is very great, insists upon

the Elizabethan worship of riches and power, and illustrates it with some striking quotations. The very poets were for this world, and glorified its rewards as if nothing better could be imagined. It was indeed a time when the old idealism of the Middle Ages had lost its power and the idealism of the modern world had not yet come into being, or at least had not established itself in the minds of men. Adventurers of the past had risked everything to defend the Cross; adventurers of the future were to risk everything to discover the truth; but meanwhile in that age of transition complete disinterestedness was the rarest of all virtues.

That, no doubt, was one cause of the magnificent effectiveness of the age; but it was also a cause of its instability. Everywhere there came a reaction against the Renaissance, the reaction of the Catholic Revival in the South and the Puritan reaction in England. Hazlitt remarks that Marlowe seems to be filled with a hunger and thirst for unrighteousness; and what he said of Marlowe the Puritans felt about the whole Renaissance. It was altogether of this world, and they would have none of it. They made a desperate effort to restore the old disinterestedness of faith, and they failed just because they were reactionaries, because they lacked the intellectual disinterestedness that was needed in the modern world.

But the difference between these two kinds of disinterestedness is only one of conditions; for they are both of the same nature and both the result of faith. In the Middle Ages men of faith believed that they knew the truth and had only to act upon it; now they

believe that the truth is infinite, and the search for
it must be endless and without limitation. Both kinds
of faith are based upon a belief in the ulterior significance of life. Only in the Middle Ages men of faith
held that its ulterior significance was known exactly ;
now they hold that it is not known, that it is not
entirely discoverable, and yet that it is the business of
man to discover all that he can about it. They are
intellectually disinterested because they have faith
in the truth wherever it may lead them, because they
value its high abstract grandeur above all material
profit whatsoever.

Spinoza said that the man who really loves God will
not expect God to love him in return ; and so the man
who has a passion for the truth will not expect to discover the whole of it. He will not be too " hot for
certainties," but will rather accept uncertainties as
tests of his faith. His is a habit of mind truly scientific, and he is the typical idealist of our age. To us
he may not seem romantic, like the idealists of the
past, but we may be sure that he will seem romantic
in the future, when perhaps some other kind of idealism
will prevail. We are proud of our material achievements, but few of them would have been possible
without that loftier knowledge, the pursuit of which
remains its own reward. Our civilisation, like all
civilisations, is founded upon the disinterested labours
of men of faith. Its obvious power and splendour are
only ornaments, which, if they become too large, may
make the whole structure top-heavy.

In every age there is a conflict between the men of

faith and the men of no faith. The issues may change, or seem to change, but the character of the combatants on each side remains the same. Often the nature of the conflict is obscured, and the men of no faith pass for men of faith, because they profess to preserve the faith of the past. Thus those who are not possessed by the idealism of our time and have no passion for the truth may seem to have a kind of piety because they do not wish their beliefs to be disturbed by this relentless pursuit of truth. They are like the artists and critics who profess a profound reverence for the art of the past because they have not enough vigour and freshness of perception to understand the living art of the present. They are not aware that the dead whom they admire were of the same nature as the living whom they condemn ; that St. Francis or St. Catharine of Siena, if they lived now, would be no more content with the past or the present than they were in their own day, but would assuredly be filled with that disturbing passion for the truth at all costs which is the idealism of our time. Men of no faith have always used the past as a stick with which to beat the present ; men of faith have always found in the present the promise of the future. Having a belief in the significance of life, they look to the future to reveal it, whether it be a future in this world or in another. The idealist of our time believes that by the pursuit of truth at all costs he can discover more and more about the significance of life, and that his discoveries, whatever their nature, will be for the good of mankind. He is not afraid of the truth, because

he has faith in it ; and everywhere he sees his enemy
in the man who has no faith in truth and fears it.

It is a significant fact that the word Atheist, as a
term of abuse, is slowly changing its meaning, and is
coming to imply one who does not care whether what
he believes is true or not. That is a sign that the
supreme faith of our time is in truth, that truth seems
to us the very essence of Divinity. A man who will
not make sacrifice for that will not make sacrifice for
any cause. He may be a decent citizen, but he cannot
be an idealist. He may help to maintain the present,
but he cannot help to mould the future. He may be
an amiable sentimentalist, but he cannot see the
romance of reality, which is the glory of truth.

BY-PRODUCTS

AMONG the greatest discoveries of science not a few
have been made by accident. Setting out to reach a
certain goal, the investigator chances in his way upon
a law, or an element, that had no place in his purpose.
The discovery is a by-product of his activity. In a
similar way, some of the most valuable resources of
industry are by-products. Not many years ago the
gas companies would gratefully give coal-tar free to
any who would take it away. Now it is sold at a
profit to farmers, to dyers, to sweetmeat-makers, to
manufacturers of scent and soap. The by-product
has become an important and lucrative property.

Modern Essays

Setting aside such accidents as the pearl, which is more precious than the oyster, human work of all kinds might be found to furnish comparable instances. When Swift wrote the travels of Lemuel Gulliver, nothing can have been further from his mind than the amusement of little boys and girls. The pleasure that some ten generations of children have taken in his book is a by-product; but it has enriched the world far more than the savage satire that was all he intended. Sir Walter Raleigh sailed the ocean for the glory of God and of his country; and, if legend speak true, he found tobacco and the potato. It would be an interesting and a beneficent work to study the history of by-products through all forms of human activity, and to record the innumerable instances in which the accident has been more serviceable to mankind than the purpose.

The value of by-products strikes with peculiar force on the mind of one who contemplates an ancient and deserted building. England is dotted with ruined castles. They were built in times of universal enmity and hatred, when lordship warred against lordship and border against border; when " the good old rule, the simple plan," was that by which men lived. Men have been driven in hundreds to death against their walls; men have been tortured to death or have rotted to death in their dungeons. Too often they were used for the oppression of the humble folk without; not a few of these mountainous piles were raised by forced labour and tyranny that might put even the Pyramids to shame. They were instruments of death, of cruelty,

and of terror. If they kept the peace, it was often the
peace of subjection, the desert where no man dared
raise his hand or his voice. Now time has swept away
their purpose. Death and cruelty and terror have
left them, to skulk in other and less grandiose haunts.
We walk under their towers, noting how proudly they
seem to march forward, how like bellying sails they
round nobly to the eye. We gather lichens or wild
plants from their stones. We dream over them in
the sunset, and rejoice in the mellow beauty of their
colour, the reflected crimson in the waters which of old
lay red with human blood. The æsthetic pleasure
that soothes and fortifies the dreamer, fitting him for
new activity in the cause of universal peace and good
will, is a by-product of a purpose immeasurably
different. So, too, with the ancient abbeys—Foun-
tains, Glastonbury, Tintern. Wordsworth wrote his
famous lines "A few miles above Tintern Abbey."
To ordinary minds the valley of the Wye, like the
country lying round any of these famous houses, is
but an approach to the ruins, so clearly do they seem
at once the key and the crown of the beauty of woods
and waters encompassing them. Whether or not he
shares the view of the monastic life which Lionel
Johnson, answering a word of Stevenson, expressed
in one of his most gravely passionate poems, whether
or not he can even go so far as Wordsworth, for whom
the monastic life

> "bodied forth the ghostliness of things
> In silence visible and perpetual calm,"

the good which the modern visitor to such places now reaps is a very different good from that for which they were built. Even the architect never foresaw nor intended the beauty of the grass between the pillars, the empty windows soaring into the moonlight, the undulant outline of the roofless and crumbling walls. The lovers, feeding upon this beauty their all-absorbing passion; the poet or the philosopher, seeing in repose and solitude new visions of freedom for the spirit of man; the very picnickers, eating their pots of honey on the grave of a dead monk and voting the ruin a "funny old place," are drawing from it a by-product of good which to those who built would seem a thing of evil.

They builded better than they knew. And seeing how much the world has gained from by-products strangely unlike the purpose that brought them accidentally into being, a cautious thinker would hesitate to condemn any form of human activity as pernicious or useless. The spirit of man is ingeniously economical. While lavish nature wastes to right and left, man, whose office it is to impose order and thrift upon nature, will make surprising use of what the lapse of time and the progress, or the change, of thought have seemed to throw out as rubbish. This is man's compensation for his ignorance of the future, of which he can see so little that he must adapt his activity closely to the present, in the trust that, be it rightly or wrongly directed, the future will find some use for it.

RHYTHM AND PURPOSE

THERE is in the movements of animals a kind of rhythmical beauty usually wanting in the movements of men, and especially of civilised men. They seem to move altogether if they move at all; and their limbs have a swing and balance which men can only attain to in the trained motions of the dance. But it is a curious fact that there is often the same rhythmical abandonment in the movements of madmen, and that in them it seems to us not beautiful but irrational. Indeed, because monkeys are so like us we often see something mad in the rhythmical abandonment of their movements. They are graceful, but we do not admire them as we admire the flight of a bird or the play of a cat. We expect more purpose in them than we find, and because of their lack of purpose they are disagreeable to us. Now there is, of course, purpose of a kind in many of the movements of animals, but, because their purposes are so few and simple, their movements are all habitual. They are not controlled or checked by the continual exercise of thought, and for that reason there is a momentum in them lacking to most of our movements. This momentum delights us, but we would not have it at the same price; and it does not delight us in human beings when we see the absence of thought and purpose in it. But the movements of human beings do give us more pleasure even than the most graceful movements of animals when

they combine this momentum with thought and purpose, as in the dance, where every movement has the
grace of habit and yet expresses something which is
not an instinctive, material want of the dancer.

Thus, with regard to this beauty of movement, we
are fallen creatures compared with animals, and yet
we have in us the capacity for a greater beauty than
theirs. Thought has broken rhythm for us, but we
may attain to a finer rhythm if we can put the same
momentum into purpose that they put into habit,
and it is our aim to do this in dancing and indeed in all
the arts. For what is poetry but a dancing kind of
speech, a speech as rhythmical and as full of momentum as the song of birds, yet at the same time as
expressive of changing and particular thoughts as
the broken speech of ordinary life? And music itself,
which in its most primitive forms is a kind of instinctive
animal escape from the fetters of language, has grown
in beauty and power through the enrichment of its
habitual rhythms with more and more precision and
complexity of purpose. Its life, as an art, consists in
this effort to express the mind of man ever more fully,
but at the same time with an animal ease and momentum of movement, so that in the symphonies of Beethoven his mind seems to be working as if it were a
bird flying through range after range of new experience
and keeping all the while the habitual beat of its un-
tiring wings.

In other arts, too, there is the same effort, though it
is not so plain to see. Painting is an art only when it
becomes rhythmical, when the painter's brush has

the same ease and momentum of movement through all its purpose of representation. But this ease and momentum must not free themselves of purpose, or the result is mannerism. The music of form must have sense in it like the music of words, or it ceases to be music and becomes mere habit that displeases us because of its irrationality.

We cannot in art, any more than in life, fall back into a thoughtless animal ease. We must attain to rhythm rather than relapse into it; indeed, we value it only when it is a symptom of purpose achieved with instinctive ease, not when it is a symptom of lack of purpose. We train ourselves, not so that we may be as simple as animals, but that we may accomplish our complex tasks as well as they accomplish their simple ones. Instinct is below us, but our reason is always trying to turn itself in a kind of higher instinct, and we recognise its success when it expresses its purpose in rhythmical beauty.

That is so in life as well as in art; indeed, all the actions of men seem to us to have the beauty of art when they are at the same time rational yet done with the ease of instinct. Good manners have this ease, yet there is always a purpose in them, and their ease is a proof that they are habitual and not assumed for the moment or to serve some particular end. So it is with good actions. They only seem beautiful to us when they are so easily done that we know they must be habitual with the doer of them; and we take delight in that ease because it is a symptom of an exalted state of being, of a mind in which will acts as

surely as appetite, just as it acts in the rhythmical but
controlled movements of a dancer. Angels have been
called the birds of God, and an angel, as we imagine
him, is a being that can do all good things as easily
as a bird flies. When we represent him with bodily
wings, we are thinking of the wings of his spirit, and
of a soaring power of action and thought for which
we have no analogy in this world except in the physical
beauty of flight.

TAKE NO THOUGHT FOR YESTERDAY

IN most novels, when one of the characters does a
wrong or foolish thing, the consequences of it pursue
him all through the book. It is one of the many delightful points about Tolstoy's *War and Peace* that its
plot is not made more exciting by this means. Nicholas
Rostov, for instance, loses a great sum of money at
cards; and from our experience of other novels we
expect that the loss will be a most important event in
this one. But it is not; it is merely something that
happens. It is wonderfully told, and Nicholas feels it
very keenly at the time; but afterwards we hear no
more of it, and we are relieved to find that Tolstoy
has not thought it necessary to contrive his plot so
that he may point a moral against gambling.

He, of course, did not write *War and Peace* to frighten
evildoers; but there are some moralists who regard
life itself as if it were a spectacle devised to frighten

evildoers, and who are always insisting, to themselves
and others, upon the cumulative effects of any wrong or
foolish action. Now it sometimes happens, of course,
that a man suffers all his life from the effects of such
an action, just as he may be crippled from slipping on
a piece of orange-peel in the street. But in both cases
he is very unfortunate, and it is not good to dwell upon
extreme misfortune, any more than upon extreme good
fortune, as if it were the rule of life. We want to see
life as it is before we draw our morals from it ; and if
we misrepresent it for a moral purpose, the morals
we draw will be themselves perverted. Thus, if we
think that in life a single false step is likely to be fatal,
we shall never learn to move boldly and freely through
it. If our morality is based on the fear of doing evil,
we shall do as little as possible. We shall be afraid
of experience, which is the best of all teachers, and at
the end we shall find that we have profited nothing
by all the dangers we have avoided.

Certainly life itself is not so intimidating as the
moralists would have us believe. The outward consequences of good and evil actions are seldom cumulative,
and, when they are, it is often through chance rather
than justice, or by reason of some convention human
rather than Divine. A clerk may steal his employers'
money, and be sent to prison for it and ruined for life.
He suffers because the offence he has committed
happens to be one that the law punishes ; but another
man may be dishonest in other ways, or commit a
hundred worse offences that the law does not punish,
without any outward evil consequences to himself

whatever; just as he may do a hundred good actions without any outward profit to himself. In fact, life, if we consider its material rewards and punishments, is altogether an unsatisfactory spectacle for the moralist; and he will only make it seem satisfactory by misrepresenting it. But life, if we misrepresent it to ourselves, takes its revenge upon us in a very subtle way, for it becomes to us what we have represented it to be. We do not escape from our mistakes and misdeeds, because we keep thinking of them. We punish ourselves in our expectation of long-drawn punishments, and the past, from our brooding upon it, gains a power over us which the present and the future cannot destroy. We forge for ourselves that tyrannous chain of cause and effect that hampers all our movements, and become the slaves of our own misconception of life.

No man can be made virtuous by the hope of rewards or the fear of punishments; life itself tells us that clearly enough if we will only look at it. If a man would be virtuous, he must love virtue for its own sake; he must aim at a certain state of being, and try to act as if he had attained to that state. Having this aim, he will always be more concerned with the present and the future than with the past. An artist, when he begins a new work, does not think of all the mistakes he has made in old ones; nor is he intimidated by the fear that, if he does something ill, it will make him a bad artist for the rest of his life. He knows that he can do nothing so well as he wishes to do it; but he does it as well as he can, and even if it is a failure at the end, he forgets it in some new work. The present task frees him from the bondage of the past, and makes him eager rather than anxious ; and so we should be eager rather than anxious over all the tasks of life. At every moment they offer us new chances ; and, though the consequences of our past actions must affect us materially, yet we can shake our souls free of them and look towards the future as if we were new-born. As regards the future, we are new-born at every moment, because we are alive, and not machines wound up to repeat the same movements for a certain space of time. We repeat nothing, for with every new experience we change ; and it is not our past actions that decide the effect of experience upon us, but our aims in the present and for the future. We, like the artist, may be sure that we shall do nothing as well as it ought to be done ; but, like him, we can learn by practice without burdening our minds with the thought of all we have done badly in the past ; for it is practice itself, the eagerness and effort of practice, that teaches us, not the memory of past mistakes. That only intimidates us, and no one who is intimidated can do anything well.

THE ASCETIC

NOWADAYS there may be men of ascetic life, but few, outside certain religious orders, make a profession of asceticism. If men deny themselves, they do so as a

rule for their family or for a cause, not for the good of
their own souls. Asceticism is no longer a method
which men commonly practise so that they may attain
to the state of being they desire ; it has been long ago
discredited among us by those who practised it as an
end in itself, either from a general fear of life or from a
self-righteous envy of the pleasures of the full-blooded.
This kind of asceticism was a mere game, like miserliness, and it is discredited because the ascetic himself
did not seem to be the better for it. He believed, no
doubt, that his spirit was triumphing over his flesh ;
but that triumph is only worth having if it leaves the
spirit free to accomplish something great. When the
spirit is so much exhausted by victory that it can do
nothing but take a rather vulgar pride in it, then the
ordinary sensual man feels that it is better for spirit and
flesh to remain on easy terms without any contention
for mastery. A compromise between them is possible
for him, but it is not possible for the higher kind of
ascetic, because the claims of both are so urgent in
him that he cannot reconcile them. He is an ascetic
because he lives more, and not less, intensely than the
ordinary man ; and his asceticism is an attempt to
live more intensely still by enriching the spirit with all
the passionate power of the flesh.

He knows that he must either do this or else allow
the flesh to be enriched with all the misused capacities
of the spirit. For there are men of great gifts who
make the opposite choice to his, who subdue the spirit
to the desires of the flesh, so that it serves them like
a subtle and cynical courtier doing the will of a licen-

tious tyrant. They make a romance of their appetites, so that lust shines like love to them and the lights of a restaurant enthral them as if they were the lights of a cathedral. Music is an incitement to their desires, and wine seems to them as divine as music; since, when they drink it, they feel like gods in a pagan paradise. Indeed, they can make a kind of mock-morality out of their pursuit of exquisite sensations, persuading themselves that connoisseurship is the whole duty of man, and that, as the universe has laboured to produce many delightful things, so it has at last produced those who are capable of enjoying them. They are the true hedonists; and the ordinary man does not understand them, nor why, with all their artful pursuit of pleasure, they are wretched. But the ascetic understands this, because he would be like them himself if he were not an ascetic, if he had not known how " to shun the heaven that leads man to that hell."

There is a Chinese proverb—Treat your thoughts like guests and your passions like children—which expresses perfectly the spirit of true asceticism. The Chinese are kind to their children; and the proverb means, therefore, that the passions should not be hated, but should be trained so that the spirit may prevail in them over the flesh. To the true ascetic his passions are part of himself, and he does not hate them, because hatred of himself or of anything else is only a spoiled passion. Still less would he wish to kill them and leave his mind desolate of them. Yet he knows that they are not occasional visitors like his thoughts,

Modern Essays

but the children of his mind, always there and always needing to be trained. Passions are not pure appetites, as children are not pure animals; they may become animal or spiritual as they are trained or spoiled, and the purpose of asceticism, when it has any purpose, is to make them spiritual. Only so can they be happy and fill the mind with their happiness and with that harmony which the spirit alone can give to them. For the spirit is not, as the purposeless ascetic supposes, a savage tyrant that would reign alone in a desolate mind; it is rather the controller of a happy family; but the family cannot be happy unless the spirit is predominant.

PHILOSOPHY AND POETRY

Everyone knows the famous lines from *Comus :*

> "How charming is divine Philosophy !
> Not harsh and crabbed, as dull fools suppose,
> But musical as is Apollo's lute,
> And a perpetual feast of nectared sweets,
> Where no crude surfeit reigns."

But most of us, however much we may admire Milton's music, cannot hear the music which it celebrates; and it seems strange to us, if we think about it at all, that a poet should speak of philosophy as if it were poetry. Nowadays philosophy seems to be the concern of philosophers, having neither the allurement of poetry nor the convincing power of science; and we

158

think of it as a difficult game, which a few experts play and a few people of curious tastes like to watch. But philosophy is not a game any more than art is a game; and those who think it is one are misled by the pretensions of those who are not philosophers.

Milton spoke of philosophy as he might have spoken of poetry for a very good reason; since philosophy, like poetry and all art, is not critical but creative, and the critical philosopher is as much a parasite upon philosophy as the imitative artist is a parasite upon art. The true artist, as we all know, makes his art out of his own experience; and that is what distinguishes him from the imitative artist, who makes his art out of the experience of others. But we are not so well aware that the true philosopher also makes his philosophy out of his own experience, and that he cannot make it out of anyone else's experience. The artist is an artist because he can communicate to us in his art the emotions which his own experience has aroused in him, so that they become our emotions; and the philosopher] is a philosopher because he can communicate to us the convictions which he has got from his own experience, so that they become our convictions. We all have emotions, and we all have convictions; but, unless we are artists or philosophers, we have not the power of communicating them and of adding from our own store to the experience of mankind.

Philosophy, since its aim is to convince, takes the form of reasoning, and nothing is easier than to reason about the convictions of others. But those who think that they will become philosophers by doing this make the same mistake as the imitative artists. The real poet makes verse because he has an emotion, caused by his own experience, which he longs to communicate, whereas the versifier makes verse because he hopes by that means to become a poet. So the real philosopher reasons because he has a conviction, arising out of his own experience, which he longs to communicate, and he can only communicate it by reasoning. But this reasoning process by itself will not make a philosopher any more than versifying by itself will make a poet. The philosopher only becomes one completely when he reasons, as the poet only becomes one when he writes poetry; but in each case there must be an impulse, arising out of experience, which fulfils itself in the work of philosophy or the work of art.

This impulse cannot be created by reasoning or by versifying, although it cannot satisfy itself without them. Something must happen to the mind of the philosopher, as of the poet—something must be conceived in it through its contact with the outside world—which is only born with the labour of reasoning. But that labour is the effect of conception, not the cause, in philosophy just as much as in art; and in both conception is the same mystery and birth the same convincing wonder. That is why Milton praised philosophy as if it were poetry; for he, being himself one who had experienced the conception and labour of art, saw that there was an equal glory in the conception and labour of philosophy.

Some may think that this view of philosophy degrades it by making it irrational. But philosophy is rational, not because it is created by the reason, but because it satisfies the reason. Reasoning is a kind of experiment that does not make discoveries but only tests them. It is the criticism which the discoverer applies to his own creation, and at the same time the creation is not complete until it has stood the test of that criticism. The philosopher, like the artist, is dual, and before he has done his work one part of him must satisfy the other. Just as the artist can only express his emotion in a form which moves himself, so the philosopher can only express his conviction in a form which convinces himself. To state it barely is not to state it at all. Indeed, a bare statement of it will seem even to him a dead platitude as soon as the first ardour of conception is past. He can only make it live by convincing himself of its truth, and to do that he must appeal to his own reason as if it were the reason of another. It is when he does this that his conviction becomes philosophy, changing from a private event in his own mind to a matter of moment for the whole world. He must have no partiality for this creature of his own brain ; for whatever critical weakness he shows towards it will become part of it, and if he convinces himself too easily he will fail to convince others. But without the private event in his own mind he can produce nothing of moment for the world, and no criticism of other men's reasoning processes will make a philosopher, however keen it may be.

It is because we mistake this kind of criticism for philosophy that we lose interest in it. It seems to us to be always destroying and never constructing.

It warns us how infinite is man's capacity for error, but never assures us of his power of attaining to truth. Indeed a great deal of it is refutation of what no real human being ever believed to be true, as if truth could only be found by the examination and rejection of all possible error. But that is not the way in which truth is sought by those who find it. They are concerned with the positive, not with the negative; and they labour to convince us that what they say is true, not that what some one else might say is false.

THE SURVIVAL OF SUPERSTITION

Superstition, like sport, is a survival from a more primitive state of society; and both have survived for reasons of the same kind. As the hunting and killing of wild animals, once the most serious business of men, has now become an amusement of their leisure, so superstition, once a grave and overshadowing fear, has now become a romantic curiosity to the frivolous mind. No doubt, to the primitive hunter hunting was just as much work as his business is now to the city man. He would rather have caught his prey without any trouble; and the modern practice of killing domestic animals in the slaughter-house would have seemed to him a solution of the whole problem of life. So too, as he had a complete belief in his superstitions, they did not interest him any more than our modern fear of disease interests us. The rites which they imposed upon him were disagreeable necessities. They did not make life seem picturesque to him any more than our sanitary precautions make life seem picturesque to us. Indeed, they were sanitary precautions dictated to him by the best science he had at his command. But now just as sport, being no longer necessary, delights men with its spice of danger and its chances of failure and success, so superstition, since it is no longer seriously believed, has a spice of playful fear in it which gives pleasure to certain minds. Their real fears are elsewhere, as the real business of men is not in the hunting-field. But these sham fears can be experienced without the constant and cumulative anxiety caused by real fears, because they are incongruous with our conception of the universe. That is the very reason why we enjoy them.

Many people are a little bored by their own sense of the relation of cause and effect ; and they like to imagine trifling escapes from it. They know well enough that the course of events is not really affected when some one walks under a ladder or helps some one else to salt. These superstitions come from a time when there was no pervading sense of the relation of cause and effect, when everything at all out of the common was regarded as the violent interposition of some unknown power. Then men felt towards a sudden calamity much as ants must feel when a child stirs up their nest with a stick. They had no notion how to prevent it ; but they thought they must have done something to make this unknown and apparently quite irrational power angry, and they hit upon something which had no connection whatever with the calamity, and resolved that they would not do it again.

There is no one now, of course, who would like to return to this conception of things, with all its helpless and overpowering fears; but it is pleasant to some minds to believe in a surviving arbitrary streak in the constitution of the universe, as we are all amused by a streak of unreason suddenly betrayed in severely rational people. Dulness often seems to be the peculiar curse of civilised life, a curse mild but pervasive; and nothing enlivens it more than a little primitive thrill. That is like an idol amid the machine-made primness of a Victorian drawing-room; and a superstition contrasts with all the flatness of routine, as the idol, with its dabs of paint and grinning roughly-carved mask, contrasts with the dull verisimilitude of photographs and the timid neatness of wall-papers.

In the real world one must look after the drains, do one's work, pay bills, take exercise, and eat wholesome food. That is the way in which we avert serious calamities, and it is a very dull way to people who cannot take a scientific interest in such things. But in this primitive world, which it amuses us to revive, one must turn one's money at the new moon, touch wood after boasting, and never sit down thirteen at table.

All these things are easy to do, and amusing, if not in themselves, at least in the absurdities which they imply. But there is one of them, the superstition of touching wood, which survives strongly enough to make us understand what superstitions were to those who really believed in them. There are many people who still fear the Nemesis provoked by boasting so much that their fear is a nervous habit, which checks the confession of happiness, even when they would make it only to themselves. This fear creeps over the bravest of men after a long spell of misfortune. When Rome was besieged by Alaric, there was a sudden revival of pagan rites in the desperate hope that they might avert the threatening disaster; and this hope was also a misgiving that the old gods were still powerful and angry at their supersession. That is the misgiving, half unconscious, which overcomes all of us now and then, and makes us afraid to believe that we have weathered our troubles, and still more afraid to say so. At such times superstition ceases to be a pleasant romantic diversion, and becomes the old intimidating demon of the past. Then we have a warning that it is not a safe plaything, that our modern security is not completely secure and our modern reason not yet entirely rational. We find that we are less civilised than we had thought, and that we had better not play tricks with our minds out of mere wantonness. But that is a lesson which we ought not to need teaching.

THE FEAR OF THE INFINITE

THE peculiar pleasure of games consists in this—that so long as we can absorb ourselves in them we seem to be shut off from infinity. We set ourselves a single definite task, to win the game ; and that task is quite disconnected from all the real tasks of life, which never can be completely performed. When a game is won or lost, there is an end of it ; and while we are playing it we need think of nothing but our play. But outside games there is no end to things so long as our consciousness of them lasts, and there is no limit to the considerations that may govern our actions. In games we make rules of our own, as if we were gods settling the laws of a universe ; and these rules are few and simple and never conflicting. But in life we have to find rules, and we know that whatever rules we find are always subject to be overridden by others. It is the dislike of infinity, again, that gives us a great part of our pleasure in stories with what we call a well-constructed plot. The essence of plot is that it has a beginning, a middle, and an end ; and the stories which men have always liked best are those in which the hero is set a definite task and after many difficulties and dangers performs it. In such stories life itself is presented as a game which the hero wins, and then there is an end of him so far as the story is concerned. It stops at the moment of his triumph, like the finale of Beethoven's Fifth Symphony, and we do not think of him beyond the triumph any more than we think of a continuation of the finale.

In life itself, again, morals may irk us in so far as they interfere with our pleasures ; and yet we are always trying to turn them into rules. There are savages who seem to civilised men to have no moral sense ; but those who know them best discover that their lives are governed by the strictest rules of conduct, that they are more conventional than any early Victorian old maid. Indeed, there is no primitive instinct stronger than that which attempts to turn life into a game, and it is an instinct which has prevented the great mass of mankind from civilising themselves. The savage may not fear pain or death, but he fears infinity so much that he will shut his mind up in a prison rather than be aware of it; and every stage of civilisation is threatened by this same fear of infinity, this same desire to turn life into a game, to make rules for it that are both definite and universal.

All men desire freedom of action, but most of them would like to have it without any freedom of thought. Freedom of thought means an infinity of choice so bewildering that no action is likely to come of it. Indeed, action itself is definite, and thought always tends to the infinite. Therefore, the desire for action must check thought if it is not to be lost in thought; and it is our instinctive desire for action, as for something definite reclaimed from infinity, which makes us put so many checks upon thought. Thought asks questions to which there is no final answer; it sets off upon a journey without an end. But every action implies, or seems to imply, a question answered; and, so long as we can absorb ourselves in it, we forget that there are any questions beyond it.

Yet thought itself is an adventure against infinity; and without it man could have no tasks except those

set him by his appetites. Behind all duty there is
thought; and duty must not disown the faculty which
created it. Duty divorced from thought becomes
lifeless, and turns into those conventions which cut
savages off from civilisation. They must have thought
enough to devise their conventions; but they are afraid
to think about them when devised. To their timid
minds there is an invincible chaos of infinity, outside
their own rules and observances, which, but for those
rules, would overcome them. But to a mind brave
with the delight of thought the surrounding infinity
is only the raw material out of which the finite can be
made. The truths to which thought attains are always
finite; indeed, perception of truth is the recognition
of the finite amid all that chaos of infinity: it is the
hearing of music where before there was only a conflict
of discordant sounds.

There is nothing so finite as music, which is the
result of choice working upon an infinite number of
combinations of sound. When we hear it we know
that the choice is not arbitrary: it seems to us discovery rather than invention; and so it is with all
the truths which the mind of man establishes. They
are not invented but recognised; and when they are
recognised the sense of infinity gives way to a perception of finite order and significance. Therefore we
may believe that infinity is only an illusion imposed
upon us by our own want of comprehension; for,
however we try to conceive it, it is always outside our
own experience. It means to us no more than an
infinite number of finite things; but the things them-

selves are all finite, and whatever general facts we discover about them are finite too.

> "The just man does on himself affirm
> God's limits, and is conscious of delight,
> Freedom, and right."

True; but the limits must be God's, not invented by man to protect him from his own fear of the infinite.

THE EGOTIST

EGOTISM, it has been often pointed out, is not the same as selfishness. A man may be thoroughly selfish yet not an egotist; and an egotist may behave most unselfishly—indeed, he may exhibit all the virtues—yet, because he is an egotist, his virtues will be acknowledged grudgingly, and no one will like him for them. Again, a man may be very much interested in himself without being an egotist. Pepys has been called an egotist, but unjustly; for his interest in himself was only part of his interest in everything else. Indeed, a man who is intensely interested in everything must be interested in himself, as being that part of reality which he knows most intimately, and which therefore surprises him most. But the true egotist is not intensely interested in anything, not even in himself. If he were, he would make himself interesting to others, as Pepys does; and that is what he never succeeds in doing.

It is the mark of the egotist that we cannot bring ourselves to be interested in anything that he says or does, unless, indeed, like Meredith, we study him pathologically as an egotist. Other men, whatever their defects, have the spontaneity and the surprises of nature ; but whatever an egotist says or does seems to be mechanical and expected. There is no novelty in our experience of him ; and we feel that he has never known any novelty in his own experience of life. Everything that happens to him is dulled by his own preconceptions ; and everything he does is in accordance with his own notion of himself, which is too firmly established in his mind to be shaken by anything outside him. He does not grow like the rest of us ; and, though time and circumstance may damage him, they do not mould him. We know that, if we meet him again after a long absence, he may be more worn, but he will not be otherwise changed ; and we shall have a curious feeling, as he talks, that he is drawing us back into his own little world, utterly cut off from the great world of reality, in which he has stayed ever since we saw him last.

It is this that makes him so depressing ; for he has the power, while we are with him, of confining us in that little world of which he himself is the centre, and of making us feel that we only exist because of our relation to him. He has this power because he himself conceives of the whole universe, and all that is in it, as existing only in relation to himself. He may be sincerely anxious to behave well to the universe ; but even while he behaves admirably to it, he does so for the good of his own soul, not from the love of anything outside him. Indeed, he is not enough aware of the reality of anything outside of him to love it. We can only love those people or things of whose independent reality we are keenly aware, and whatever we love for its relation to ourselves we love with self-love. But, for the egotist, he himself is the only complete reality, and other things only acquire reality from their relation to him.

This is not a metaphysical position with him, but a disease; for, whatever tests of reality metaphysicians may devise, there is no doubt that we are most healthy in mind and body when we are most conscious of the independent reality of others. Indeed, with every disease of body and mind our sense of that independent reality is weakened, and we tend to see the world outside us only in relation to the painful reality of ourselves. In perfect health that reality ceases to be painful, and we are no more aware of it than of other realities. We fall into our place in the universe, and perform our part in a relation which is not made by the supremacy of our own selves.

For the egotist all relations are made by the supremacy of his own self. It is not necessarily that he thinks himself better than other men or that he is determined to impose his will upon them. It is simply that they do not exist for him as he exists for himself. He is alone in the universe; for he cannot find companions of his own reality, and for that reason he is often uneasily concerned with the relation between himself and others. He may have a very exacting

sense of duty, and set himself tasks of beneficence for
which no one is grateful just because they are tasks
set for the good of his own soul. In these tasks he
seems to do no good either to his own soul or to any one
else; for he performs them without understanding or
joy, as if he were a dog trained to do tricks. The
nearest he can ever come to joy is in self-satisfaction,
which is a very poor substitute for it; for when we
feel joy we are not satisfied with ourselves but in love
with the universe.

Therefore we need not envy the egotist his self-
satisfaction, and we need not even resent it. Our
natural impulse is to take him and shake him out of
it; to explain to him, with all the force of language at
our command, that we exist just as much as he does
and are not dependants upon his superior reality.
But that very desire to assert ourselves proves that
we, too, are not quite free of egotism. If we were,
we should only pity his disease. Indeed, we do pity
it in its extremes, when it becomes madness, for then
its nature is plain to everyone, and everyone forgives
its unpleasant results. But all egotism is disease in
that it consists of a want of normal apprehension
which may increase until the sufferer from it is unfit
for freedom. It is a want, not so easily defined as a
want of hearing or sight, but none the less real; and
we all suffer from it more or less, just as none of us
has perfect sight or hearing. There are times when
the reality of others grows faint to us, compared with
the exorbitant reality of ourselves, and when we
therefore become unpleasant both to others and to

ourselves. The egotist is always in this state, and he is so used to it that he often ceases to be unpleasant to himself. It is as unkind to grudge him this poor consolation as it would be to grudge their consolations to the deaf and blind.

UNORTHODOXY

THERE is an unorthodoxy in smaller matters and another in matters of the greatest import, and one must distinguish between them because they usually have very different causes. The minor unorthodoxy may be only a sacrifice of smaller to greater things ; and even wise men may take some pleasure in it as a protest against the sacrifice of greater things to smaller. There are so many matters in which one may have a high standard that it is necessary to choose among them, and the world is always apt to keep its standard high in material things rather than in spiritual. Thus, cleanliness is a most important point in the orthodoxy of the well-to-do. Indeed, it is far more necessary to social success than godliness, and many, to whom it is a pleasure, regard it in themselves as a virtue. So there have been saintly men, in modern times and in England, who have insisted even in their practice that cleanliness comes after godliness. They have fallen far short of the orthodox standard in this physical matter, but only because of their greater orthodoxy in spiritual matters. Again, the Bohemianism of

artists is a minor unorthodoxy, and often there is some
protest in it against certain minor orthodoxies. The
Bohemian of sense, being poor, would rather live
freely and easily than imitate the extreme domestic
order of the rich. He does not care if his home is a
little untidy provided he can enjoy himself in it, nor
if his hospitality is happy-go-lucky so long as he can
afford to be hospitable. But if he goes further in
revolt and likes disorder for its own sake, then his
unorthodoxy has begun to pervert his judgment, and
he becomes himself a proof of the value of that minor
orthodoxy which he despises. So a saint who rolled
in the mud to show his contempt of cleanliness would
prove thereby the value of cleanliness, not only to the
body, but also to the mind. He would prove that the
minor unorthodoxy may lead to the major, which is
the very point that he began by disputing.

Cleanliness and order in themselves are good things,
and there is nothing to be said against them except
when things still better are sacrificed to them. But
the major unorthodoxy consists in saying that good
things are bad in themselves, and when once you
have said that about small matters you may soon say
it about great. The rebellion of the major unorthodoxy
is not particular, but general. It is the rebellion of
an anarchist rather than of a revolutionary, and would
destroy the whole fabric of human judgment rather
than correct minor errors in it.

Very often those who fall into the major unorthodoxy
are not aware what has happened to them, and do not
carry it very far. Indeed, no human being has ever

been thoroughly consistent in it. Even Milton's Satan, though he cried "Evil, be thou my good," not only displayed virtues, but recognised them as virtues. He paid that unconscious homage to the moral order while he was professing complete rebellion against it.

But the major unorthodoxy consists, not in conscious rebellion against the whole moral order, but in ignorance of the fact that it is all of a piece. One cannot pick and choose among those things which the common consent of mankind has determined to be virtues or vices, and say "I will call this virtue a vice or this vice a virtue." To say that is to deny the whole moral sense, and not only that, but the whole power of judgment in humanity. And when you do that you are denying your own moral sense and your own power of judgment also. We may all differ, even from the general opinion, about the value of particular actions. We may say that they seem to us symptoms of a certain virtue rather than of a certain vice ; but that is quite different from saying that a certain virtue is really a vice. Even if it be a minor virtue, it is the moral sense, and not mere convenience, that makes it one ; and the moral sense must stand or fall by the whole body of its judgments.

In every age there is a tendency to the major unorthodoxy on some one point or another. And at that point we can see the peculiar vice and danger of the age. Our present unorthodoxy is very like the unorthodoxy of the Renaissance. It consists in denying the value of humility and pity, those peculiarly Christian virtues which to Nietzsche seemed to belong to a slave morality. They were, he said, hostile to other virtues, such as courage and resolution, which seemed to him the cardinal virtues; and therefore he called them not virtues, but vices. On this point one can appeal against him to common experience. We know that humility and pity are not inconsistent with courage and resolution; indeed, that they often produce acts of the greatest bravery. But further than that, we know that the same causes which make men humble and compassionate also make them brave and resolute. It is true that a man may be compassionate without being brave, or brave without being compassionate. That is merely because of the imperfection of human nature. But instinctively we admire his bravery less if he is not compassionate, and his compassion less if he is not brave. Each of those virtues arouses in us the same kind of emotion, and they arouse it most strongly when they are combined.

And that emotion which virtues arouse in us, being always of the same kind, is the reason why we call them virtues. If you deny the justice of the emotion at one point, you must deny it at all. But no one has ever succeeded in doing that; and the major unorthodoxy, whether of individuals or of whole societies, has always been finally condemned because of its inconsistency.

Modern Essays

ORTHODOXY

THE word orthodox is commonly used nowadays, like the word worthy, with a slightly contemptuous sense. If we say that a man is worthy, we imply that he does not interest us; and if we say that an opinion is orthodox, we usually proceed to disagree with it. Yet there is nothing contemptuous in the original meaning of either word. To be orthodox is merely to be right; and the shade of contempt which has darkened the word implies, not that it is wrong to be right, but that we have grown a little impatient of a certain kind of rightness. The orthodox, in this sense, are the people who hold the right opinions but have not come by them honestly. If they are right they do not deserve to be right; and our impatience is not really for the opinions which they hold, but for their manner of holding them. There are some, of course, who think that an opinion must be wrong if they dislike the people who hold it. They are pragmatists, very likely without knowing it, and judge opinions by their effects upon character. But what they take to be the effect of opinion on character is often really the effect of character upon opinion. Truth in the abstract is simply truth; but directly men begin to express it or to act upon it they seem to colour it with their own peculiarities. One man will turn a flashing truth into a platitude, while another will turn the dullest platitude into a flashing truth; and the manner in which we express truth or act upon it depends upon the manner in which we have come by it. We may say in fact that truth is "not negotiable" between mind and mind. A man must have a title to it, he must have earned it, before he can pass it on. So, we use orthodox in the contemptuous sense of a body of truths which are held by those who have no title to them, and which therefore we refuse to accept from them.

All this does not apply to scientific truths. They do not become platitudes by repetition, nor have we any contempt for those who accept them, or act upon them, at second-hand. The reason is, not that a scientific truth differs in its nature from any other kind of truth, but that it only holds its place as a truth because it is continually confirmed by experience. Many scientific truths are not confirmed by the experience of the mass of men, because it is only the few who have sufficient knowledge to experience them. The rest of us accept the opinion of those few because we trust them to believe nothing that is contrary to their experience. It is indeed a point of honour with the scientific conscience to believe nothing that is contrary to experience, and all men of science are interested in maintaining that point. But moral truths are concerned with facts that are within the experience of everyone, and with regard to them we are all men of science, or ought to be. True, we must often act upon them without having tested them by experience, for, whereas no one is forced to be a man of science, everyone who continues to live must be a man of action. There is an incessant choice forced upon

178

us in matters of conduct, and in making our choice we must often follow moral principles which we accept merely because they are generally accepted. In doing this we should be thoroughly aware that we are acting, not upon our own moral convictions, but upon the moral convictions of others. Those convictions may be right, but we can take no credit for their rightness; and, because they are not ours, we have no power of communicating them to others. Indeed, if we utter moral opinions without moral conviction, they sound like platitudes, and arouse that prejudice against the truth which is so commonly expressed in the contemptuous use of the word orthodox.

We owe to the moral law a larger duty than that of mere obedience. Our duty is to discover it through our own experience and to strengthen it by means of that discovery. The moral law is always being threatened, and not least by a blind obedience without conviction, which provokes an equally blind rebellion against it. Our proper relation to it is not that of a subject to a despot, but of a citizen to a free State who helps to make the laws which he willingly obeys, and who will therefore neither obey for the sake of obedience nor rebel for the sake of rebellion. The one success in life worth having is to obey a moral law joyfully, and that can only be done by those who have discovered it for themselves. This does not mean in the least that they must discover a new moral law, but only that it will seem new to them if they discover it.

We know how great poets can give novelty and splendour to what would seem a commonplace uttered in other words. That is not, as people often put it, because of their power of language, but because it is a surprise rather than a commonplace to them. Though they know, like the rest of us, that something has happened a million times before, their own experience of it is not dulled by that knowledge. They go through life making discoveries, and their language is quickened by the ardour of discovery. So it is with those who discover old moral laws for themselves. For them those laws are truths, not merely guide-posts, and they have all the beauty and surprise of truths suddenly apprehended. They believe them, not because others believe them, but as we believe in beauty when we see it ; and this belief of theirs has a contagious power. No one sneers at it as orthodox, no one calls the expression of it a platitude. Truths only become platitudes when they are already platitudes to those who express them. It is the mind that dulls them, and the mind may also refresh them with the ardour of its welcome.

THE CRAVING FOR SOLITUDE

In the midst of the facile life of London and other great cities one constantly encounters people who express a fervid desire to escape from the fancied toils of their multitudinous environment. Sometimes they crave for nothing more than a cottage in the country, or yearn to sit, like Thoreau, beside a pond. Others dream of the immensities of the sea, or of wanderings amid deserts, or of a lonely sojourn among tall mountains. They think with envy of explorers marching through African forests, of men ice-bound in the long brooding night of the Arctic, of silent frontier sentinels, of space and free air and solitude. They rebel against the innumerable pettinesses in which they are enmeshed. The tyranny of letters, the oppressive distractions of newspapers, the inconsequence of callers, the exactions of social engagements—all these things trouble and depress them. They cherish the belief that if they could only cut through the nets which entangle them they would lead more free and happy lives. Their fancies are almost invariably imbued with the idea that modern life imposes far more nervous strain than civilised mankind has ever known before. The telephone, the penny post, the motor-car, the taxi-cab, the myriad contrivances which were invented to make existence smoother and easier, are all supposed in some mysterious fashion to produce nerve exhaustion and mental irritation and weariness. Men and women do not cease to use these conveniences, but they affect a desire to be emancipated from their thraldom. There are no taxi-cabs in the desert, it is argued, and no telephones at sea. Could one fly to such spacious desolation, it might be possible to think. Cut off from the rest of humanity, one should discern the purpose of life more clearly. In London one cannot think, and life seems to be a purposeless round of trivialities which will never lead to soaring vision.

We have sketched a very common frame of mind, which is nevertheless exceedingly misguided and unwholesome. If men and women really want to think about the larger problems of life, they can gratify their wish without retreating to a desert or a mountain-top. The only real necessity is a sufficient intensity of desire within themselves. The capacity for thought is independent of environment. If a man's daily pursuits seem to prevent thought, it is because he has become the willing and eager slave of unprofitable habits and desires. The idea that modern conveniences are nerve-exhausting is probably a delusion fostered by too much ease. Since the death of Ruskin it has not been so customary to decry railway trains. They are accepted as a matter of course, and we can perceive that stage-coaches in the days before Macadam must have been far more trying to the nerves. In due course, when the proper perspective is reached, we shall admit that the telephone saves many weary steps and many irksome letters, and that motor-cars and taxi-cabs do not deserve to be the theme of countless lamentations. It is not these accessories of life which prevent thought. Rightly used, they should furnish more time for thought.

Again, though existence appears complex enough to us, it must have seemed far more nerve-exhausting to the Dutch in the days of Spanish oppression. An Italian citizen of the fourteenth century, who lived in constant dread of seeing his home destroyed by ruthless *condottieri*, and found neither safety nor quietude from the cradle to the grave, would have thought modern

London a place of holy calm. Those who have travelled much in the jungle and the desert know very well that deep reflection is not necessarily stimulated in the waste regions of nature. The mind is more often absorbed in the daily routine of the journey, in the constant struggle with the elements, in the sense of fatiguing toil and the necessity of procuring food. The camp-fire at night merely invites slumber, except in novels ; the starry heavens are only scanned for presage of rain. Such rovings are rather a mental anodyne—they produce action, but not reflection ; the time for thought is not during travel, but in long moments of retrospection afterwards. A ship is the most populous of man's inventions, and a long voyage generally deadens thought instead of prompting it. Nor have the romantic pictures of hermits seated amid marble ruins on sunlit capes, or perched on high among the majestic peaks of the Himalayas, any relation to reality. Not thus is mental detachment and spiritual exaltation attained. The best-known Indian devotee of modern times, who became a *sanyasi* after a brilliant administrative career, sat in his own house in a humble saffron robe and received his friends.

The author of a recent popular novel takes as his theme the modern craving for escape from the absorptions of civilised life. He sends a young couple, tired of the distractions of London, into the icy wilds of Labrador, to " face God, and clear things up " in their minds. There was no need for them to go to Labrador in search of God or in hope of clearer minds, as the

writer no doubt perceived when he rang down his
curtain upon their obviously eager return. It is
noticeable that this sort of experiment always exercises the greatest fascination upon those who have no
knowledge of the wilderness. Communion with nature
can be enjoyed with as much facility in Regent's Park
as on the banks of a frozen river ; and clarity of thought
is not assisted by a broken leg or a conflict with a lynx.
The craving for thoughts that bring light need impel
no one forth into the waste places of the earth ; the
means for its assuagement lie ready to hand. Life
need not be overwhelmingly complex, though it re-
quires a rigorous determination not to make it so.
The way to freedom from useless preoccupations is
not to flee from them, but rather to face and excise
them. There is no man so fettered that he cannot
find time to " clear things up in his mind " if he is
sufficiently resolute ; but he will not achieve his purpose best by becoming a cenobite.

We have spoken of the professed desire for solitude
as modern, but the truth is that it is not modern at
all. A century ago Wordsworth was bewailing that
" the world is too much with us " ; in the early centuries of the Christian era monachism was a fashionable
cult ; at one time there were as many anchorites in
the deserts of Egypt as there were men in the cities.
The tendency is as old as humanity itself. There is
in this respect only one marked difference between our
own and preceding eras. In the days of St. Jerome
vast numbers of men and women really sought
solitude. The modern man talks a great deal

of the complexity of existence and the need for reflective inanition, and then whirls onward in a taxi-cab.

TWO KINDS OF OPTIMISM

THERE are two kinds of optimism, the practical and the theoretical, and the difficulty is to combine the two. The practical optimism, often preached by successful men of business because it is one secret of their success, is the optimism of the early bird hunting for a worm and finding it. He has no doubt that worms are worth finding, or that it is his business in life to find them. And so long as he does find them in plenty, and enjoys them and digests them well, he lives in the happy expectation of finding and enjoying and digesting them. For him life is a succession of worms which he makes his own, and he does not concern himself with the worm's feelings or with the nature of a universe in which worms are food for early birds. His private problem is the only one for him, and so long as he solves it he approves of life and expects to approve of it. If he were to consider the worm's feelings, or to ask himself questions about the nature of the universe, he would not find so many worms. He would, in fact, be wasting his time and lessening his enjoyment. Philosophy, therefore, would lead him straight to pessimism ; and, if he considered philosophers at all, he would no doubt attribute their pessimism, when they were pessimists, to the fact that they had chosen a wrong way of life and were naturally disgusted with it.

But man, either because he has a soul or because he has developed certain unmanageable and irrelevant faculties in the struggle for life, cannot, however early he gets up, content himself entirely with the thought of his earliness or the success it brings him. Among men, besides the early birds, there are also the philosophers who observe the early birds and comment upon them, and who have even taught the early birds to comment upon themselves.

For the real early bird there exists nothing but the particular—at least, that is the common belief, although birds sing as well as hunt for worms. But for man there exists also the universe and the necessity of relating his particular business to it. There are men, of course, who never feel that necessity. Success after success comes to them, as worm after worm to the early bird, and they take delight in one venture after another because they expect to win them all. That is their kind of optimism—a belief that the universe is of such a nature that they will succeed in it. They may go further, and think that their success is a proof both of their own virtue and of the just and rational nature of the universe. In that case they are merely early birds with a power of expressing their own satisfaction in the form of a theory. But most of us, even if we are successful in life, cannot be thus theoretically satisfied with our success. For we differ from the early bird on one important point from the very start. He has no choice of businesses, for worms are always

his business, and he has only one way of getting them.
But for us there is an infinite diversity of businesses,
and we may have an infinite diversity of faculties.
We compare one business with another, and ask ourselves not only which we can do best, but also which
is best worth doing. So we cannot attain to optimism
merely through confidence in our own success. For
optimism to us means, on the one hand, that there is
something in life that is worth doing and, on the other,
that we ourselves are doing it.

The belief that there is something in life worth doing
depends upon a conviction that life, universal life,
means something for the infinite future, whether it
be pleasant or unpleasant at the moment; and the
stronger our conviction is of this continuous and
prophetic meaning of life, the more apt we are to ask
ourselves whether our particular business has its part
in this universal meaning. The more we are optimists
about the universe, the harder we find it to be optimists about ourselves. A man may feel convinced
that St. Francis and Michelangelo and Beethoven were
occupied with great matters, or rather in their diverse
ways with one great matter of eternal moment; and
he asks himself how far he, in the work which he does
to earn his living, is also occupied with that great
matter. It is not that he has an egotistical desire for
their fame, for he knows, if he knows anything, that
fame is a by-product, worth having but not to be
aimed at. What he desires is their sense of the significance of his work and the cumulative power which
only that sense can give. This is not a matter of

187

happiness or unhappiness. The greatest men are subject to extremes of both, just because they have given their hearts away to life. But they consent to both, as a lover consents to them, and express their passionate consent in all their thoughts and actions. How is a man not gifted with these powers but possessed by their faith to express it also in all his actions and to confirm it, as they did, by that expression ? That is the problem for optimists, and it is more difficult to solve it than to be an optimist; more difficult still, perhaps, to remain an optimist when you have failed to solve it. Indeed, that is the last heroism required of the ordinary man ; and it may be that in preserving his optimism through this failure he is, without knowing it, winning the success of the great ones and giving to his life that significance which all the while it seems to lack.

CYNICISM OLD AND NEW

CYNICISM is not fashionable nowadays either as a philosophy or as a method of humour. We no longer take any pleasure in talking scandal about human nature—at least we leave it to men of science to do that, and they do it without any of the gusto of the humourist. The old humorous cynicism was a mischievous attack upon human prestige and dignity. When men were supposed to be a little lower than the angels, there was some fun in showing their likeness to the beasts. But when that likeness has become a commonplace of science, and man has been dethroned, by his own thought, cynicism is merely platitude and has as little liveliness about it as copybook morality.

No doubt there was a time when the saying that no great man is a hero to his valet seemed both wicked and surprising. But that epigram has been expanded into stout volumes about the connection between genius and epilepsy, which make us almost thankful that we have not the misfortune to be great. It was possible once to be cynical about Joan of Arc, to prove with some vivacity that she was an impostor supported by priests and statesmen for their own ends, and wit could sparkle over the contrast between this imposture and the splendour of the national legend that it produced. But when medical science takes the matter up and tells us that Joan herself was only the most hysterical person in an age of hysteria, then we have no spirit left to be cynical. Rather we become hypochondriacal about humanity and are tempted to feel that a rest cure is the proper remedy for all its conflicts and glories, for all the illusions which the flesh imposes upon a non-existent spirit.

There is a kind of confidence and security in cynicism which we lack nowadays. Doctor Johnson said that any man who depreciated himself only did so to show how much he had to spare. After all the discoveries and theories of the last hundred years, we do not feel that humanity has enough to spare for cynicism. We have scientific formulæ for all the old jokes that were made against it, and so the jokes sound to us too much like truth to be amusing. There was a kind of cynical rage in men like Swift which came of disappointment. He felt that he had been taken in by the pretensions of humanity, and he reviled them as impostors who might be chastened by the revelation of their own baseness. To him also the animalism of men was mere perversity. His yahoos were bestial by their own fault, and therefore lower than beasts; there was something devilish in them which he hated and which he hoped to punish by making them hate themselves. But if Swift were alive now he would leave the description of yahoos to conscientious naturalists such as Zola. His genius, however fierce and unhappy, could not ease itself with cynicism, for it would find no pretensions in humanity to destroy. Nowadays a Swift, writing as he wrote, would have all dull men on his side, and that would be intolerable to him. His rage could not vent itself in scientific platitudes, and it would have therefore to find a vent in some kind of rebellion against them.

Samuel Butler was the last of the cynics; and his behaviour proves how difficult it is to be a cynic in the modern world; for he saw that, if he was to escape platitude, he must always keep his temper with mankind. To fall into a rage with humanity was to confess that you had harboured obsolete expectations of it, that you were making discoveries which everyone else had made long ago. He therefore remained perfectly calm, and treated human beings as if they were rather amusing creatures who might enjoy themselves as much as he enjoyed them if only they would not take anything too seriously. He was,

indeed, the first to be cynical about modern science;
for he refused to take that any more seriously than
any other human product. He smiled at our modern
discoveries as much as at our old pretensions. Thus
he pointed the way out of the depression which those
discoveries have caused. For after all, if we take our
own discoveries about ourselves too much to heart,
it must be because we have an excessive opinion of
our own wisdom. It is conceit that makes us sure of
our own insignificance, for if we were not conceited
we should be sure of nothing. We are still trusting
in our own understanding of the universe even when
we give ourselves a very low place in it. He therefore was cynical about that understanding; and in
this ultimate cynicism of his there was the germ of
a new mysticism—a mysticism which smiles at the
self-confidence of man when he declares himself to be
nothing but matter. If we have a very low opinion
of ourselves we are not likely to be right, for there is
an evident inconsistency between that opinion and our
confidence in it. So cynicism begins to comfort us
when there remains nothing discomforting for it to say.

THE PLAIN MAN

WE all know the plain man very well by hearsay, and
most of us are a little afraid of him, because he is
always used as a weapon against us. "That is not
the kind of argument," we are told, "that is likely to

appeal to the plain man." The argument may seem to us a good one, but we must put it away from us and find another that is likely to appeal to this plain man. There he is, powerful because of his numbers and his robust if rather unimaginative common sense, waiting to receive all our best arguments with the fatal words— "As a plain man, that does not appeal to me." But where is he? We are always meeting people who know all about him, who can tell us what he likes and dislikes, and what he thinks, or rather how his common sense makes it unnecessary for him to think at all; but he himself, though he is said to be the greatest power in the country, is a power more mysterious than the Grand Lama of Tibet. The Grand Lama is in his palace somewhere; he dies, and another succeeds him; he has his Ministers and his officials. But the plain man, we are told, is everywhere, in trains and omnibuses, in the House of Commons and at all political meetings. He reads all books and newspapers; everything, in fact, except poetry. He likes all the plays and pictures that no one whom we have ever met does like; and he has opinions upon every subject, only they are not opinions that we have ever heard expressed by any individual. In fact, powerful and respected as he is, he seems to have no friends, except perhaps among other plain men; for those who know most about him can never introduce you to him. Even in a club smoking-room, where he abounds, they cannot say, "Here is Mr. X, a plain man; try your argument upon him and see what he thinks of it." At least if they did, Mr. X would certainly take it very ill.

Modern Essays

This much is certain, that no one is ever a plain man to himself. The people who begin a sentence with the words "I am a plain man" are not to be trusted. Mark Antony said that he was no orator but a plain, blunt man; and he said it in the course of the most eloquent and artful speech in literature. Iago, too, pretended to be a plain man, and he was less honest even than Mark Antony. The plain man whom we all fear and respect but do not know is not like them; but what is he like? Even those who appeal most confidently to him describe him only by negatives. They can tell us of a hundred fine things that he despises, but of none that he admires. They warn us that he will misunderstand everything we have to say to him; but they cannot say what he will understand. He is supposed to be entirely absorbed in his business, rather like the economic man; indeed, he usually is a man of business, only we do not meet him among men of business any more than among poets or artists. The individual man of business may tell us with an air of confidence what the plain man thinks; but he is not the plain man himself because he is an individual, and it appears that the plain man, whatever he may be, is never that. He is rather a composite photograph of a large number of individuals, chosen on no principle and with all their positive characters neutralised by the composition. He is an idea that we get of the world when we are afraid of it, like that idea of his audience which a nervous speaker gets when he looks vaguely at the mass of faces in front of him and feels that they are all hostile and all unintelligent.

He is, in fact, an idol like those idols which savages set up to personify all that they most fear and dislike, and which they hope to deceive by means of their own self-deception. We all of us, when we look at the world and see that it is very different from what we should wish it to be, assume that it wishes to be what it is. Therefore we make to ourselves this image of the plain man, who by his wishes controls the world ; and we persuade ourselves that he exists and that there is something admirable in him, just because he is so entirely unlike any real men, with their uncertainties and shortcomings, whom we have ever met. He at least knows what he likes, though no one else knows it ; he never falls short of his aim, because he never has one. He has made the world and is content with it, and all who are not content with it are not plain men.

Now, as a generalisation, he might have some value if he were not a complete perversion of the facts. The shortcomings of the world are the result, not of the wishes of the plain man, but of the failures of all those real men who are not plain. And he in his mysterious and intangible power is merely an abstraction of the weaknesses of all of us. The world is not what it is because he has made it so, but because we have failed to make it what we wish it to be. It is as if we were all pulling in different directions and believed, therefore, that some unseen but positive power was resisting all our efforts. This power we call by the name of the plain man ; and he does not exist. He is merely a personification of the neutralising effect of all our differences. Therefore, when we address him, we speak to no one ; and we are likely to succeed better if we address ourselves to men as we know them, who, however much they may differ among themselves and from us, are never plain men.

AMATEUR AND PROFESSIONAL

ONE of the most discouraging things about life, for those who like to be discouraged, is the fact that it is impossible to be an amateur and a professional at the same time. If we are to do anything well, we must learn systematically how to do it ; and this systematic training often makes us do it in such a manner that it seems to be not worth doing. Take, for instance, the case of the orator. He ought to be a man who speaks out of the fulness of his heart, who has a message to deliver so urgent that words rush to his lips like servants eager to do the bidding of his mind. Unfortunately he cannot make words thus obedient to him, unless he is always speaking ; and when he speaks for practice he cannot do so out of the fulness of his heart. His business, in fact, is to pretend to be an amateur when he is really a professional ; to counterfeit inspiration so that he may be able to profit by it when it comes ; and the worst of it is that he cannot learn how to profit by it except through counterfeiting it. But this process of counterfeit is not good either for his own soul or for his art. He may, by expressing

the great emotions, come actually to feel them. The
words and tones and gestures of righteous indignation
may hypnotise him as well as his audience, but the
emotion itself, induced by this process, is coarsened by
the means that induce it. Like the speech, it is made
to order, produced not by events but by the demand for
it ; and anyone who is not hypnotised himself can see
the tawdriness of it. Yet the professional's success
depends upon his not seeing it. He must become professional in his mind as well as in his methods ; he
must sway himself with his own sham magic, if he is
to sway his audience. And when the sham magic
becomes real to him, then his " nature is subdued to
what it works in, like the dyer's hand."

These words prove that Shakespeare himself, the
seemingly omnipotent artist, felt the danger and injury
of professionalism. When he wrote them he had not
yet attained to the glory of the amateur with complete command of all professional accomplishment.
Indeed, there has never yet been a man on this earth
who has attained to it ; and we may conceive of heaven
as the only place in which practice is not needed to
make perfect, in which perfection is not marred by
the routine or insincerity of practice. The angels,
perhaps, can make music as easily as they can think ;
for them inspiration and accomplishment may be one.
But every man who is very accomplished in his own
craft is either a bit of a pedant or a bit of a charlatan ;
and without this accomplishment, with its taint of one
or the other, we cannot do anything that is worth doing.

It is the dream of the recluse to withdraw himself

from the professionalism just as much as from the sin-
fulness of the world, to live in the music of his own
spontaneous thought like the angels. But even he
becomes a professional in his very withdrawal. The
perfect amateur, if he existed, would be the natural
man exercising his faculties on all sides as easily and
as beautifully as a flower grows; but the recluse
refuses to exercise most of his faculties, so that he may
the better exercise a few of them. And he is professional in this very refusal.

Yet the ascetic way is perhaps the best means of
escape from the grossness of professionalism. The
man who wants little of other men will not coarsen
himself to please them. Rembrandt became a greater
artist all his life because he became more and more
ascetic in his art, and in the finest works of his old age
we see nothing to satisfy the lust of the eye. When
he painted them he must have been a man who did
not seek in reality for any of the pleasant things that
most of us seek for in it. Disregarding all its obvious
beauties, he treated it as a raw material which he
invested with the beauty of his own moods. Having
forgone all hope of worldly success, he made no effort
to please the world with his professional power of representing what the world liked. And thus in the last
stage of his mastery he was freer from the professional
taint than any other artist known to us. He was,
in fact, a saint among painters, one who could reveal
the best wisdom of his art to anyone who would seek
for it, but not one who would try to sway a congrega-
tion with fluent eloquence.

Modern Essays

And yet, in this imperfect world, there is a need for
fluent eloquence; and very great men have been content to practise it, and to sway thousands with something coarser, something less true, than their possible
best. They have made some sacrifice of themselves
to professionalism, but the best of them have always
known when they have made it and have suffered from
the knowledge. It is when men enjoy their professionalism without any misgiving, when they delight
in their own technical mastery as if it were the inspiration of the divine amateur, that they are in danger of
becoming charlatans. We cannot be angels in this
world, and if we pretend to ourselves that we are, we
lose even the promise and interest of our own human
imperfection.

MYTHS ANCIENT AND MODERN

Men have always enjoyed making myths about the
origin of things. For instance, nearly every race or
tribe of men has its myth about the origin of evil;
and before men became scientific these myths took the
form of stories about particular people who had names
and characters of their own. But now that we have
become scientific we have changed all that. It is
impossible for us to take this old kind of myth seriously,
although we assume that it was taken quite seriously
in the past. We have therefore made a new kind of
myth of our own about the origin of things which is

more in accordance with our own scientific spirit; and we expound it, not in short stories or poems, but in very long books full of argument and evidence.

And yet, in spite of this difference of form, the new myths seem to be produced by just the same impulse as the old ones. Primitive man saw evil everywhere about him, and he asked himself how it began. In answer to this question he made a story about its beginning. The scientific investigator sees religion or the drama equally prevalent, and asks himself how it began; and in answer to his question he makes, not a story, but a theory. But he usually assumes in his theory, just like primitive man in his story, that man in some remote past had some particular reason for worshipping or for making plays which does not exist now. No one now would look for a particular reason for either of these activities. Men make plays because they want to make them, just as they make love; and they worship because they feel the need of worship. But in the remote past they began to make plays because they wished to pay respect to the memory of a hero, or because they were very much interested in the fact that vegetation died down every year and revived the next; and this fact also induced them to worship.

It may be that three or four thousand years hence, when, after a long intervening period of darkness, there is another age of enlightenment, some one will produce a theory of the origin of pictures. Then no doubt there will be multitudes of pictures painted because people like pictures; but the theorist will, of course, find another reason why they were first painted. In the remote past, he will say, there was a religious age in which men thought about nothing but religion. That was followed by a commercial age in which men thought about nothing but commerce, and every institution and activity had a commercial origin. Then, for instance, a gold coin was called a sovereign, a conscious acknowledgment of the universal supremacy of commerce. This age was described by those who lived in it as the age of advertisement. For some thousands of years—how many is uncertain— advertisement consisted merely of the recommendation of wares by printed words which almost entirely covered all buildings. But at some period, not yet precisely ascertained, some one, probably a vendor of soap, introduced a crude representation of a piece of soap into one of his printed advertisements. The innovation must have aroused great interest and largely increased the sale of his soap. Then, some generations later, under the stress of competition, another soap merchant produced a representation, no doubt very imperfect, of human beings washing themselves with his soap; and this was the real beginning of pictorial art and also the explanation of the remarkable prevalence of the nude in the pictures of several succeeding centuries. But it was a long time before painters achieved their independence and ceased to be merely the servants of tradesmen. The first artist to do this is said to have been one Millais, who gained so much fame by an advertisement of soap in his youth that he ventured afterwards to paint pictures with no advertising purpose; but this may be merely myth. At any rate certain artists, although associated with the advertisement of certain wares, had also reputations of their own, such as the tailors' and the dyers' painters, Andrea del Sarto and Tintoretto. It is unknown how long a period elapsed between them and the completely independent artists, such as Michelangelo and Cimabue. But it appears that in the works of the former there was no trace of their advertising origin except the nudity of his figures, while the latter freed his art even from this last commercial convention. Indeed, it is probable that in the age of Cimabue the advertising purpose of art was forgotten altogether, and that erroneous myths were prevalent about its religious origin.

Now, if a theory of this sort were presented to us about the art of our own time we should be surprised, not so much at its errors of detail as at the notion that any theory should be needed at all. We make pictures as the palæolithic men made them, because we like them. And this liking for pictures always has existed and always will exist. There is a perpetual impulse to produce pictures which is not started by any particular pretext, but exists in the nature of man; and if our memory of the past could suddenly be wiped out of our minds we should begin to make pictures again, just as they have been made in the past. We cannot explain why we have this impulse to make pictures, but we know enough about ourselves to be sure that any explanation which finds some accidental and external cause for it is absurd. But when we come to consider primitive man we do not judge him by what we know of ourselves, but by theories which learned men make for us. In fact, we behave just like primitive man himself, and our theories are produced by the same impulse as his myths—by the desire to find a starting-point which never existed. We shall not be really different from him until we learn to put our own myths into our books about comparative mythology.

CASTLES IN THE AIR

THOSE who build castles in the air are occasionally spoken of by more matter-of-fact persons with brutal and noisy derision, but oftener with a kind of tender pity which they find, not unjustifiably, far more exasperating. It implies so complete a misunderstanding of the builders' frame of mind. They are supposed to live in a vale of disappointments; but, if they be out and out workmen with a love of their art, they do in fact nothing of the kind. Long before one castle has actually fallen, sometimes even before so much as a tell-tale crack has appeared in the walls, they are planning the foundations of another on a larger and more gorgeous scale. When the crash ultimately comes, it is unheard for the din of cranes and hammers already hard at work again. We have it on Sam Weller's authority that to take to building houses is " a medical term for being incurable." And very fortunately this is, *a fortiori*, still more true of castles.

It is not, however, this implication of a life made up of disillusionments that is the most difficult to bear. Rather is it the suggestion that those who indulge in day-dreams are so besotted as to believe that they will all of them come true. This is at once a slur on their intelligence and on their ability to play their own game properly : it shows that the sympathetic and stupid creatures who make it could never acquire the rudiments of the game if they were to try for a thousand years. As long as the player is trammelled by doubts and wonderings whether anything so beautiful could ever really befall him, he must almost of necessity curb his fancy and turn sadly back from some glorious flight ; but, once he has as much as half admitted to himself that he is moving in the realms of fantasy, he can soar away to heights unknown.

Perhaps by playing the game so wildly, and treating it so entirely as a game, we may increase our own immediate pleasure at the expense of some possible indirect benefits. By frankly divorcing our dreaming from our practical ambitions, we may be robbing ourselves of a valuable encouragement or incentive. On the other hand, it may be argued that the practical and the dreaming or castle-building parts of us should deliberately be kept in separate compartments from a workaday point of view, and, whether right or wrong, most people probably do so.

The youthful barrister may dream in his many leisure moments of the glories of silk or of dispensing small witticisms from the Bench to a sycophantic audience; but these images do not occupy his mind when he finds himself in a stuffy County Court, with an obtrusively new blue bag, £1, 3s. 6d. marked on his brief, and his learned brethren ostentatiously wondering who he is. At that ghastly moment his ambition does not soar far beyond the not making a fool of himself, and possibly, in the very dim future, the receiving of another brief from the same client. It is only at night, when the dreadful revelry is past and he has overcome an inclination to bury his head, as did Mr. Winkle, in the sofa cushions, that the old beatific visions return to hearten him for the morrow and nothing to do in chambers.

Putting altogether on one side the delight that they give in the making, it may well be a question whether any material profit is to be derived from castles in the air; whether, to take our previous example, that young gentleman would not have employed his evening better in noting cases rather than in seeing in the fire the picture of himself in a full-bottomed wig. It is extremely difficult to obtain sufficiently reliable statistics by which to decide the point. If we are ordinarily unsuccessful people we are probably too much inclined to think that many of the most successful of our acquaintance can never in their youth have built castles at all. The intensely prosperous appearance of their waistcoats to-day appears somehow to our short-sighted eyes prohibitive of such a notion. Even in the case of those whom we are willing to credit with some ability in that line, we yet believe that their

castles must have been rather dull ones. We picture
one of their buildings to ourselves as having something
too much of real bricks and mortar about it, echoing
the perpetual whirr of lifts and guarded by a commissionaire in the basement.

But if we turn up our imaginative noses at that
imposing and eminently practical edifice we are in
fact convicting ourselves of a lack of imagination,
We ought to understand that, for a certain type of
builder, this type of castle is the most splendidly
fantastic that could exist, and full of all sorts of exciting beauties that we cannot see. There is a hopeless
difference in architectural taste, but the spirit in which
that pile was built may have been at least as romantic
as ours.

"I TOLD YOU SO"

THERE is a class of persons whose wisdom is the envy
and despair of all their less gifted fellows, upon whom
they sit in judgment. Not merely is the correctness
of their verdicts strangely accurate, but they are pro-
tected at all points by the heavy armour of conscious
rectitude against any retort from the judged and
condemned. They live, in consequence, tranquil and
well-ordered lives incapable of disorganisation by those
turns of fortune which affect lesser folk. In fact,
other people's failures supply the principal interest of
their existence, and the motto of the clan is " I told
you so." Their justification, if ever they sought one

for their assumption of the judicial robe would be their own success in life. They are self-elected censors of the failures by right of their own prosperity. For the wise man is a successful man according to his lights. Success with him is a purely negative idea. It means the absence of failure. It is not well, therefore, to plead with him in defence the great historical truth that the world's successes have been founded upon failures. The plea would only confirm his suspicion that your mental capacity was not merely deficient— ample proof of which lies in the present failure, as duly foreseen and prophesied by himself—but actually impaired.

While argument in such a case means waste of time and temper, it is better to bear meekly the triumphant " I told you so " and the recital of steps which ought to have been and cannot now be taken. For the majority of us, the imperfect majority, no more irritating phenomenon can be met with among all the minor worries that are the real burdens in life than this form of retrospective wisdom. The vice, for such it is, is practised largely by relatives and ex-tutors who claim to " take an interest " in us, or by persons who have so little to occupy them that they are obliged to direct, from the security of pensioned ease, their critical attentions to others.

Theirs is the negative righteousness which irritates and does not help. In the statement that they told us so is implied the assumption that the advice they gave, probably unasked, was more than right ; it was bound to be right. We, the admonished and exasperated, know that their advice was mean and pusillanimous, that it was and is wrong, and that only chance has clothed it with an appearance of truth. If it was not wrong, then, at least, it was obvious and a platitude conveying some such sentiment as "look before you leap."

Tennyson has bequeathed to debating societies an undying topic of discussion in observing, not without courage, that it "is better to have loved and lost than never to have loved at all." Though Tennyson is a "safe" poet, and eminently the favourite of our wise people, this view of life is anathema to them. It is, indeed, almost better never to have run the risk of losing than to be compelled to hear some merciless Eliphaz forcing upon us his coldest consolations. The soreness of the failure itself is infinitely less than the smart of that unilluminating and arrogant comment "I told you so." Its sting lies in its futility. Purists in orthodoxy such as these take no risks. They wait till time has "proved them right." It is part of their passion for correctness. Then, when failure is evident and hope is low, they come with their parrot-call to raise our wrath and damp our courage, and to inform us that they always said we had chosen the wrong career.

Failure is a formidable thing chiefly because of these prophets, whose reputation feeds upon the failure of others. Boys who have run away to sea have sometimes become great men after and confounded the family critics. Other boys have run away to sea in just the same spirit of enterprise and ambition but have remained obscure or sunk in the world. The burden and bitterness of failure is doubled by the consciousness of what their friends and relations will say and are saying. They cannot return to face it. The instinct is rather to lie hid. The appeal to the prodigal which promises him through a newspaper advertisement that if he will return " nothing will be said" proves daily how strong and universal this feeling is. The first meeting of reconciliation is in fact an experience which both the prodigal and his parents know to be awkward and difficult.

In justice to the wise people, whose valuable and gratuitous advice so many of us rejected long ago, it must be said that it is hard for any man to repress that acutely uncomfortable feeling of self-righteousness as he tries to welcome unaffectedly the prodigal home. It is reflected in the peculiarly self-conscious look of the good dog who watches the castigation of the bad one. This feeling finds its fullest expression in all who are not unpleased that the misfortunes of some one who has rejected their counsel should bear witness to their wisdom ; but it is a feeling for the rest of us to keep a tight hand on. Samuel Butler relates how, in answer to a little Italian girl who asked for centesimi, he replied " You don't want any centesimi." He adds that, as soon as these words fell from his lips, he knew he must be growing old. So when a friend in whom we " take an interest " retails his misfortunes to us, it is well if we do not retort that we told him so. For the moment that these words tremble on our lips we can judge that we had grown, not necessarily old, but futile and narrow.

Modern Essays

BOOKS IN WAR-TIME

A MEDIÆVAL fancy that still lingers, ghostlike, on the more lonely seashores, such as that Breton one so tenderly described by Renan, is the legend of the submerged city. It lies out there barely hidden under the waves, and on a still summer eve they say you may hear the music of its cathedral bells. One day the waters will recede, and the city in all its old beauty be revealed again. Might this not serve to figure the actual condition of literature, in the nobler sense of the term, submerged as that seems to many to be by the high-tide of war ? Thus submerged it seemed, at any rate, to the most delicate of our literary artists, who was lately accounting for his disused pen to an aggrieved friend. "I have no heart," he said, "for literature in this war ; we can only have faith that it is still there under the waters, and will some day re-emerge."

It is a common discouragement. *Inter arma silent* so many things besides laws. Nor is the discouragement merely a mood. Obviously there is economic ground for it. Publishers are coy. After all, books are written to be read, and the great public is spending its shillings on other things than books, or, at the best, on books that are no books. It may well seem to our more sensitive authors that a khaki-clad or khaki-minded world has no use for them. Some of the younger ones have thrown authorship to the winds and gone to the front ; indeed, one poet at least died

a noble death there. But most of them are sedentary
men with a bad habit of being well on in middle-age.
These may yet join a committee or a volunteer corps,
become special constables, or otherwise " do their
bit." The one thing they cannot do is their own
proper work of authorship ; they have no heart for
it, and, if they had, the world, they fear, would have
no ear for it.

Apart, however, from this professional aspect of the
matter, tragic enough though that is for the authors
themselves, there is fortunately no truth in the idea
of a sunken literature. A function of the spirit, it
can never be submerged or, indeed, so much as touched
by war or any other external thing. It is an inalien-
able possession and incorruptible part of man. We
do wrong to despond about it, unconquerable as it is,
bomb-proof against all possible Zeppelins, immune
from any poison gas. It should be a private consolation to-day to every man with the slightest tincture
of letters that he carries always with him a magic
talisman. For in the very thick of that most violent
of human activities which we call war the contemplative spirit passes unscathed, and is not to be balked
of its natural satisfaction. It is over there in the very
firing-line, snatching a moment for some cherished
pocket-volume, or finding ingenuous utterance in the
songs and nicknames of the men. So far from being
exact is the common dichotomy of " active " and
" contemplative " men.

Roughly, however, the distinction will serve. Indeed
there are many men who seem to be without that

indispensable condition precedent to all art and literature which the language of our Western Allies calls
the *vie intérieure*. They exist only in the society of
other men, and, left alone, vanish into the void, like the
Vawdry of Mr. Henry James. That temperament is
in luck to-day, when Mr. Churchill tells us, and none
can gainsay him, that the whole nation must be
" socialised." But the naturally contemplative man,
on his active side not debarred from responding less
readily than anyone else to the patriotic call, is in
better luck still. For amid the loudest din of arms,
after the extremest tension of that effort to live and to
do for something not ourselves which war imposes
upon us all as at once a duty and a spiritual purifica-
tion, there comes the inevitable moment when we must
live within ourselves and be cast upon the resources
of our inner life. It is in that moment that we get
glimpses at the city that in our haste we had thought
submerged, and hear its cathedral bells sounding clear
and high above the waters. Socialisation in that moment is seen to have its complement and its auxiliary
in the purest and best individualisation. It is our
own individual spirit that we realise, our own im-
prisoned consciousness that we set free in literature,
and yet without egotism, without any blunting, indeed
with the sharpening, of our zest for the great business
wherein we are all now called to co-operate.

And, just because of its individual appeal, it is idle
to prescribe what literature men should read. The
choice may have infinite range, from Homer's *Iliad*,
" which is the best," to the last verses in *Punch*, from

the new Sherlock Holmes to Pomponius Mela *De Situ Orbis*, which learned work Johnson perused when journeying with Boswell in the Harwich coach. Johnson, by the way, it was who declared, in his preface to his Dictionary, that " the chief glory of every people arises from its authors." This has a grave air, perhaps, at the moment, yet from the moment it gets its best proof. For in a reeling and blood-stained world literature maintains inviolate its inward and spiritual grace, never to be reached by any enemy whatsoever, because its kingdom is within us.

ON TABOOS

TABOOS do not exist only in savage countries. We have them ourselves, only we are not aware of them except by comparing past taboos with present. But our taboos are the more absolute because they are unconscious. They work like a law of nature, and yet they are artificial; for often they do not exist, or are much weaker, in other countries. Thus in England there is an absolute taboo, imposed not by any law, but by a common, almost instinctive, consent, upon any boasting about good looks. The best-looking man in England would rather boast of anything else in the world than of his beauty. Indeed, if anyone spoke to him about it, he would be more embarrassed than if he were accused of some disgraceful crime.

It may be said that this is not a taboo, because it is

not irrational. That is true; it is not well to boast about anything, but there is an almost superstitious intensity in our aversion to boasting upon this particular point. We may dislike boasting on any subject, but we do not feel that a man has made an intolerable exhibition of himself if he boasts of his cleverness, or his wisdom, or his athletic powers, or his social position, provided his boasting on these subjects is skilfully veiled. We may smile at his vanity and at the indirect manner in which he gratifies it, but we do not feel that he has put himself outside the pale, that we have all a right to pity and despise him because of it. If, however, he were to boast of his good looks, no skill or indirectness in his boasting would mitigate his offence. He would embarrass us, as if he had suddenly shown that he was mad, or at least that he was different in kind from all the rest of us. And yet there is no reason why we should despise him for this kind of boasting more than for some others. Very likely to a Frenchman or an Italian it would seem less offensive to boast of good looks than of riches; and if a Frenchman boasted to us of his good looks, we should only smile at it as a French peculiarity—a proof that there is something artificial in our own taboo, that we apply it only to ourselves and in our own social atmosphere.

But we have also a taboo, less absolute, upon the display of emotion—a taboo which hardly existed at all for our great-grandfathers. If a man shed tears in public nowadays, unless he had some overwhelming excuse for it, we should think that he either was foolishly emotional by nature or that he ought to

undergo a rest-cure. But our ancestors, at the time
of the Napoleonic wars, men who were certainly not
weaker than ourselves, used to shed tears freely in
public, and for reasons that would seem to us quite
inadequate; and the French still do so, although we
no longer believe that they are womanish or call
them Froggies. This is another instance of a taboo
exercised unconsciously and for reasons that we
cannot explain, a taboo that might at any time cease
to act with some obscure change in our sense of
propriety.

Such an obscure change, again, has laid an increasing
taboo upon those moral judgments which our ancestors
a hundred years ago uttered so freely. Jane Austen
was not a writer naturally interested in morals, but
her characters are always passing moral judgments
upon each other with what would seem to us intolerable priggishness. A Darcy of our time would make
a point of ignoring morals in his judgments of other
people. He would disapprove of the Bennet family
for any reason rather than the reasons which he gave
to Elizabeth. Indeed, when he tells Elizabeth what
he thinks of her family he is incredible to us, not merely
because he is rude or tactless, but because his reasons
for his disapproval are all moral. He talks of them
as we should hardly talk now of a family that was
flagrantly disreputable.

One could discover reasons for all these taboos.
We dislike boasting about good looks because it is
so shamelessly asinine; it reminds us of a peacock
spreading his tail. We dislike weeping in public be-

cause it seems to take an unfair advantage of us, like the incontinent pathos of bad art. We dislike moral judgments in ordinary conversation because our morals at present are changing, and many moral judgments provoke us to an argument more lengthy and serious than we wish to begin at the tea-table. But these reasons will not quite explain the instinctive embarrassment, the sense of shame, that we experience when a taboo is violated. That is something primitive in us, a collective uneasiness that we inherit from the time when there were religious reasons for all social rules, when any breach of them was a kind of sacrilege which tainted all who were present at the breach. The collective uneasiness remains, though the religious fears are gone; and it imposes upon us taboos which are inexplicable to those of a different time or country, inexplicable even to ourselves.

THE LOVE OF MONEY

THE love of money can hardly be the root of all evil, for it is only one perverse passion out of many. But there is a kind of decorum about money which makes the love of it peculiarly dangerous, since it conceals from the lover the nature and effects of his passion. If a man wants too much food, he is evidently greedy. If a woman wants too many clothes, she is evidently vain. But money is not a thing, like clothes or food, that can be enjoyed by itself. It is only a means of

getting the things that can be enjoyed ; and so greed
for money is not direct greed, but indirect. It is a
civilised means of conducting the struggle for life,
which to a great extent conceals from those who use
it the ugliness and the animal nature of that struggle.
It is, in fact, a kind of diplomacy, politely conducted,
behind which there is war ; but the diplomats often
do not see the war. They deal only in documents,
scraps of paper ; and they are not aware, except at
second hand, what all these documents, and the
struggle about them, mean to the mass of men. The
rich man who is greedy for money does not put it to
himself that he is greedy for all the things that money
will buy. Although money keeps its actual power,
and is prized for that, he manages in his own mind
to divorce it from its real meaning. It becomes to
him a symbol of something much finer and more
romantic than it is. It inflames his imagination and
the imagination of a great part of the poorer world
too, as if it were not merely a means of buying material
things, but a personal quality in the man who possesses
it. Money, it is said, can be used for great and noble
purposes, which is true ; but the man who is greedy
for money does not want to use it for such purposes.
Often he does not even want to buy an inordinate
number of material things. His greed has become
abstract and romantic. It is greed for a symbol,
forgetful of what the symbol implies.

And this greed for a symbol spreads among people
not otherwise greedy, who do manage by means of
money to engage ruthlessly in the struggle for life

without ever being aware that they are red of tooth and claw. The decorum of money wraps itself round them, and hides from them the character and the results of their own greed. They see only lists of securities; they do not even see heaps of gold ; and, even if they do engage in a quarrel about money with some one else no less greedy for it, there is no open scrambling and clutching, but only a law-suit decently conducted, which may cause decent ruin to the loser that the winner never sees. All he knows is that he has got judgment in his favour, which means, of course, that he takes a certain number of material things from his opponent. But it does not mean that to him. To him it means a kind of religious justification, giving him a moral as well as a legal right to own the money he gets through it.

That we do unconsciously reverence money more than the things we get with it is proved by two curious facts. You can give a man anything except money without affecting your relations with him ; and a man's dependents may steal many things from him without calling it theft, but they know always that taking money is stealing. Evidently, then, money is more sacred than any other kind of material possession. But why ? It only differs from other material possessions in that it is a means of getting them, that while you have money you keep your power of choice be- cause you have not yet chosen. So if you give money you only give the power of choice, and if you steal money you steal the power of choice ; and this power seems to us more sacred than any of the things that can be chosen. We do reverence the man who has a great deal of this power, just because he has not yet chosen, and because, perhaps, he might choose nobly or generously. But we may be sure that, if he is greedy of the power, he will not choose nobly or generously— in fact, that the man who can ennoble money is he who cares very little for it.

The war makes all these things plainer to us than they were in time of peace. We now see greed for money as it is; and we no longer reverence the rich man because of what he might do with his money, since we have other tests forced upon us than these possibilities. We value a man for what he does, not for what he might do; for his actual personal qualities rather than for his possessions. In that we are like people on a sinking ship, for whom all the customary social values are destroyed, and a man is a man only if he proves himself one. To us now the private who wins the Victoria Cross is really a better man than the millionaire who cannot sleep at night for fear of bombs. The money test is, for the time, almost abolished. We know by our own experiences at last that a man may be poor, not because he is a fool or a weakling, but because he cares for other things than money.

But shall we remember this when peace comes again? Men commonly apply this money test, not so much because they are base in their own desires as because it is easy to apply. We know by hearsay when a man is rich; we have to find out for ourselves whether he is simple and kindly and brave. But our judgments are worth nothing to ourselves or anyone

else unless we make them for ourselves, unless they
are based upon what a man does rather than on what
he has; and there is nothing which hinders us so
much from exercising our own judgment as the reverence for money. It hides from us our own greed and
the greed of others. It spreads a fog of decorum
where there ought to be no decorum at all; it makes
us think there is peace where there is a sharp material
war. And this war, not purely material, opens our
eyes to the nature of the other. It will have one good
result at least if it keeps them open.

NAUGHTINESS

WHEN we think of childhood as a happy state, utterly
passed away and irrecoverable like a vivid dream,
what is it that we chiefly miss from it in our manhood?
What is the change we have suffered which cuts us
off from it so sharply, as if it were the change from sleeping to waking? We can tell ourselves of many things
we have gained—wisdom, experience, dignity, responsibility, and what not; but we never look in these for
what we have lost. We assume that childhood had
its illusions which are gone; but we do not ask whether
we may not have contracted illusions from which childhood was free. Dignity, for instance, we have now,
and we lacked it when we were children, when we were
carried screaming up to the nursery in a fit of naughtiness. Indeed, we never are naughty now; but how

often we wish we could be! There, at any rate, is one definite thing that we miss from childhood now that we are grown up; and what have we got in return for it? This dignity which turns our naughtiness into wickedness and changes our punishment into something as uninteresting as the offence itself. For naughtiness was at least exciting, and so was the penalty for it. It came and went like an April shower; it was a mood that we indulged without seeking a reason for it. We had no dignity that made us try to justify it; but now, when we feel naughty, we know that we are grown up and must find a reason for our naughtiness, and it is just that finding a reason for it which turns it into wickedness. It is well, of course, never to be naughty at all; and we all pretend to others and even to ourselves that, being grown up, we never are and never can be naughty.

There is a time between childhood and manhood when we would rather feel wicked than naughty, when we do, in fact, take great pains to turn our naughtiness into wickedness and are affronted if we still receive the blessed, easy punishments of naughtiness. That is the fatal period in which we grow used to our loss of the privilege of childhood so gradually and so willingly that in after years we are not even aware that we have lost it. We learn in time not to take a pride in being bold and bad; but we do not try to regain our childish sense of the naughtiness of ourselves or of others. The child can be naughty itself because it sees only naughtiness in the sins of other children. It lives in a world where fits of naughtiness

happen like thunderstorms and are soon over and done
with. But we, having learnt the habit of moral indignation which makes the naughtiness of others seem
wickedness to us, have also lost the power of being
naughty ourselves. We wonder at the forgiveness of
children ; but they forgive so easily because they think
there is not much to forgive. We are unjust to them,
perhaps, or cruel, and afterwards we seem to ourselves monsters of iniquity. But to them we have
only seemed naughty ; it is as if we had suddenly
pulled their hair or broken their toys. They do not
know that we have justified our naughtiness to ourselves ; that we have found it necessary to think ill
of them before we punished them ; and that what
rankles afterwards in our minds is the injustice of this
justification. A child does not need to think ill of his
sister before he pulls her hair. He just pulls it because
he feels naughty ; and if she pulls his hair it is for
the same reason. These things happen and you are
smacked or put in the corner for them, and there is
an end of them.

Well, when we are grown up we cannot be smacked
and put in the corner for our naughtiness ; and so we
have invented other punishments for it. But that is
no reason why we should deceive ourselves about it.
The best way to deal with naughtiness is to know what
it is ; and there are some happy people who keep the
childish privilege of naughtiness all their lives, because
they themselves know when they are naughty. When
they do what would be called wicked in anyone else,
they are said to act just like a naughty child. And the

reason is that they have not enough sense of dignity to seem wicked to themselves. Their behaviour is naughty, like their state of mind, and they do not pretend that it is anything else.

The wicked man professes to act on principle, and it is this deliberate perversity in him that makes us call him wicked. So most of us, even when we are naughty, are ashamed to betray the symptoms of naughtiness. We preserve a calm and dignified demeanour, and for that reason our naughtiness, so concealed and suppressed, is mistaken for deliberate wickedness. If only we could be naughty obviously and without this pretence of dignity, people would shrug their shoulders at us, feel their own superiority, and condemn us no more than they condemn a child. And we ourselves, having vented our naughtiness, should quickly be ashamed of it and, as it were, put ourselves in the corner.

But we could not treat our own sins thus lightly unless we were ready so to treat the sins of others. If we are to have the privileges of childhood, we must be as forgiving as children are; and we must detect mere naughtiness even when it tries to give itself the dignity of wickedness. Saints cannot be wicked, but they know well enough that they might easily be naughty; and that is the reason why mankind seem to them to be all naughty but pardonable children.

Modern Essays

THE KNOWING MAN

To be knowing is not the same as to know, for we know particular things, whereas the knowing man is knowing about everything, and whatever he knows is a secret. He tells it readily enough; indeed he tells it often to those who do not want to hear it. But he was always either told it as a secret or else he learnt it by means of his own peculiar experience and sagacity. Thus, if there is a scandal he knows the uttermost truth about it, which is something far more surprising than anyone suspected, and it affects the highest in the land. Indeed this uttermost truth is so dangerous that he looks round uneasily and lowers his voice when he tells it, as if he were afraid that informers were dogging him, or at least that there was a reporter lurking about to take shorthand notes of his disclosures. And yet you may be sure that he has told it to everyone who would stay to listen, and that it is growing and will grow more and more startling with every repetition, until the truth about a new scandal supersedes it.

But when there is no scandal notorious enough to exercise his mind, he is knowing about the things which he has learnt through his own peculiar sagacity, as, for instance, where you can get the best claret at 25*s.* a dozen, or the best cigars at 25*s.* a hundred—the price in each case varies with his economic station; which is the best cheap, or dear, restaurant in Paris; which is the most improper French novel lately pub-

lished ; or, if he is a man of high culture, which is the
last Italian Primitive to be exalted above the best but
one. For men are knowing about all kind of things,
from a public-house to a religion. It is a chance of
circumstance or station what they may choose to
be knowing about; but the attitude is always the
same, and it always arouses the same wonder in the
unknowing.

No one ever dares to ask the knowing man how he
learns all his dark secrets, and we may be sure he never
stops to ask himself. His energy is exhausted in
telling other people, so that he has none to spare to
question himself. A hint of gossip in a newspaper;
we may suspect, grows in his mind until it is a long
circumstantial story told to him by an influential
person who singled him out alone to be burdened with
it. He may never tell this lie in so many words, but
he implies it and more by his manner ; and it is this
manner, with its intensity expressing so much more
than he really means, which gives him his keenest
delight. He is not commonly ill-natured, nor does he
spread scandal about the great from envy of them.
What he enjoys is merely the sense that he is communicating a dark secret, and he does it so dramatically
that, if you are good-natured, you will pretend to be
startled by what he tells you. But do this, and he
will grow more and more furtively confidential, until
you wonder whether he knows all the time that you
know that he is a liar. And this wonder will become
embarrassing at last as he looks at you with that
searching glance that has discovered all these secrets,

Modern Essays

and draws closer and closer to you so that he may matter the last, most dangerous, secret of all in your ear. Then, perhaps, the sense of monstrous unreality will grow too strong for you, and you will start up and say that you have an appointment and are already late for it. And as you leave the smoking-room of the club, for it is there that knowing men usually make their disclosures, you will see him already looking about for some one else to confide in.

When two knowing men fall in with each other there is always a laborious competition between them. They do not commonly give each other the lie, for to do that would be to blow upon the whole business of knowingness; but they rush in to supplement each other's revelations, each taking it for granted that what the other tells is matter of common knowledge, and that he alone knows the exclusive and really dangerous secrets. So they do not like each other; and, if only they would think, they would see that no one else likes them very much either. For their assumption is that the rest of the world is outside the circle of exclusive knowledge; and they always have the air of telling us that we should know if we were real men of the world such as they are.

The man of learning does not fret our vanity, for he is a specialist; and the more learned he is the less does he seem to insist upon his learning. But the knowing man's pose is that he knows more than all the rest of us about what we should all like to know. He professes, in fact, to be a learned man of the world; and it is that profession that makes us all a little impatient. For every man at the bottom of his heart likes to be thought a man of the world, and dislikes to be surpassed in worldly knowledge. Besides, the knowing man always knows already anything that you may tell him, and is able to supplement it in detail. Your conversation is to him merely a pretext for his own. He makes the running all the time, and would feel himself defeated if he ever seemed to be learning instead of teaching. And yet you know that some chance remark of yours may be the germ of a long revelation that he will make to his next listener. He does know some facts, and must get them from somewhere, though he is always familiar with them the moment he has heard them.

And this familiarity is the penalty of his pose; for, however much he may move others to wonder, he can never allow himself to wonder at anything. Since he knows whatever he is told, everything is in the past for him; and surprise would be a humiliating confession that he has been overtaken by news and is living for once in the present. He is the very opposite of a child for whom everything is news; and he makes you feel as he talks to you that there is no spring or morning in life, but that everything happened yesterday and has now the smell of stale cigar smoke about it.

Modern Essays

TWO KINDS OF FAMILY FEELING

PROBABLY every family large enough to be called a
family at all has a family feeling by which it distinguishes members of the family from the rest of the
world.   By this we do not mean natural affection, but
something independent of that, however closely it may
be connected with it; the same feeling, only more
intense, which for an Englishman distinguishes other
Englishmen from foreigners.   But this family feeling
takes two extreme forms, which again are quite independent of family affection.   In one form every member
of the family thinks that the family is likely to be right
in everything; in the other he thinks that it is likely
to be wrong.   Some families are determinedly self-
confident; others are morbidly diffident.   The latter
feel always that the rest of the world have a secret of
sagacity and right behaviour that is hidden from
themselves.   This kind of family feeling may begin
very early in life.   There are children who feel that
their parents are not as other parents; that they
have not learnt the proper trick of worldly behaviour,
that they dress and talk oddly, and that anyone can
take advantage of them.   They may all the while
love their parents passionately, but for that very reason
they criticise them the more, and pity while they
criticise.   And to them, as they grow older, their
family seems a forlorn and defenceless group in the
midst of a hostile and far more competent world.   This
feeling is more common in clever families than in

227

stupid ones, for real ability in youth is apt to be over-conscious of its own defects, and often success in later years removes it. At any rate, the diffident family is better liked by the rest of the world than the self-confident one.

There is something peculiarly irritating in a family that has turned itself into a mutual admiration society, and which judges the rest of the world always by its own standards and always finds it wanting. Such families are often praised for their affection, even while they are disliked; and yet there is a good deal of vicarious egotism in the high opinion they have of each other. They believe firmly that any member of their family can do anything better than all the rest of the world; and so, if they are a family of influence and power, it is a point of patriotism with them to dedicate all their members to the service of their country. That is how they put it to themselves; and they are so sincere in their belief that it is unfair to call them jobbers. If William has not yet found a job, they feel that William is being wasted with all his family abilities. The Empire has need of him, and they combine together to satisfy the Empire's needs. If it is pointed out to them that William seems to have no particular claims or qualifications, they are not at all dismayed. They know William better than anyone outside the family can know him; and they know that, being a member of the family and sharing all its hereditary and acquired advantages, he is more than competent to fill any place that may be con-venient to him. Families of this kind, because of their determined unanimity, have a great advantage in the world. They do not get all that they want, but by constant practice they learn a method of procedure which usually obtains for them many more places than they deserve.

And yet this kind of family feeling has its dangers for the family itself. A complacent family, when it has been long powerful and successful, often acquires an almost ant-like clannishness which perverts its sense of right and wrong. Some member of that family may be, within the family, an acknowledged ne'er-do-weel and nuisance; but in his dealings with the world he is still supported, and no outsider has any rights against his hereditary privilege. The family knows, perhaps, that he is quarrelsome; but if he quarrels with an outsider the outsider is in fault. It knows he is incompetent, but however many places he may lose he is still fit for any new one that offers; and the more of a burden he is to the family, the more it feels the country's obligation to support him. There is this to be said for these complacent families—that they are very slow to disown any of their members; but whether that is from affection or from an unwillingness to believe in a family failure it is difficult to say. At any rate, if you are a ne'er-do-weel it is best to belong to one of these complacent families. They will give you every chance, at other people's expense if not at their own; and though, within the family, they may make you feel that you are its basest member, they will still imply that you have some undefined superiority over the rest of the world.

THE SILLY SEASON

ONE can imagine a Platonic dialogue in which Socrates would prove, gently but firmly, that the silly season is the only wise one, since it is the time when people give up wrangling over things of the moment and discuss matters of universal importance. Indeed, in Athens the silly season seems to have lasted all the year through, and Socrates was always ready to take part in its discussions. The Athenians killed him at last ; but we should probably treat him even worse, for we should ignore him. We tolerate such discussions only when they are carried on by specialists—that is to say, by people who talk a peculiar jargon and have, or seem to have, a great command of statistics.

Socrates was no specialist. He talked just like any-one else, and appealed to the common experience of mankind when he discussed matters of which everyone has experience. His object was to discover the truth about such matters. We despair of that, and try, if we ever think of them at all, to accumulate out-of-the-way facts about them. We do not discuss the immortality of the soul as if it were a matter that immediately concerned us, but inquire what savages think about it. We are more eager to learn about the marriage customs of South Sea Islanders than about the opinions of the ordinary British householder upon marriage. So, when a time comes at which the ordinary British householder is allowed to give his opinion upon such matters in the newspapers, we call it the silly season, meaning either that no one but a fool would express his opinions upon them, or that the ordinary man's opinions are not worth having. We consider that no one should discuss matters of universal importance unless he has some special qualification for doing so. We want experts in everything, and we have the oddest notion of what constitutes an expert. Thus we would rather hear a bachelor talk about marriage, if only he can give us a multitude of figures, than a man who has just celebrated his golden wedding. The one has a great deal of second-hand information about marriage in general, perhaps; the other has some first-hand experience of his own marriage in particular. Yet the first would be called an expert; and the second, if he wants to say anything, must wait for the silly season to say it.

It may be that the wisest people do not readily discuss such matters nowadays. There are many interesting subjects on which " the kings of modern thought are dumb "; and we may suspect that they are dumb just because they do not wish to be implicated in the discussions of the silly season. They wish always to speak with the authority of the expert, and they are aware that no man can be an expert upon many questions which are of the greatest moment to mankind.

If this is their motive for silence, there is some mock humility in it. It is likely enough that Socrates, if he lived now, would engage eagerly in the discussions of the silly season, and would write long letters to the papers proving the most unexpected things. He would not be afraid for his dignity, nor of the suspicion that he was trying to advertise himself. He would enjoy a debate about the great questions of life too much to ask himself whether the other parties to it were worthy of him. He would also be curious to know what the ordinary man thought about such questions; and that, after all, is the main interest of the discussions of the silly season.

Though we are supposed to live in a democratic time, we hear very little of the opinions of the ordinary man upon most subjects. In books the experts and specialists usually have matters all to themselves. Philosophy, especially ethics, is everybody's concern; yet philosophers take pains to use a language intelligible only to other philosophers. They use as many technical terms as if they were chemists or mathematicians. The very words philosophy and ethics seem meant to warn the ordinary man off those subjects. Milton insists that philosophy is not harsh and crabbed as dull fools suppose; but the philosophers do all they can to make it harsh and crabbed and to isolate their speculations from the common ideas of mankind. The professional thinker, since he is always thinking, is apt to think himself away from all experience. But the ideas of the ordinary man, however commonplace they may be, are provoked only by experience, just as folksong is provoked only by emotion; and they have the same quality of spontaneity and simplicity.

The philosopher, therefore, should not despise the

discussions of the silly season; nor should he be impatient if opinions expressed in them seem to be commonplace or vague. Whatever kind of philosopher he may be, it is his business to know the mind of the ordinary man; for, unless he knows that, he is in danger of losing his sense of the relative importance of things. The worst defect of the ordinary man in discussion, nowadays, is that too often he is not content to express himself like an ordinary man. He tries so hard to assume the airs of a professional thinker that his meaning is lost among a number of misused technical terms. If only the correspondents of the silly season would write as they talk, their letters would be the most interesting things that ever appear in the newspapers. They might sometimes amuse unintentionally; but they would still be amusing, like the conversation of Doctor Johnson's old school-fellow who had tried to be a philosopher but had given it up because he was too cheerful.

It is a sad fact that nowadays everyone is afraid of the superior person, and that is the reason why so few people can write well. They do not understand that a man's language must be fitted to the quality of his thought. If he has ordinary things to say, he should express them in ordinary words. If he is not used to abstract thinking, he should avoid abstract terms. They will only distract him from saying what he has to say, or persuade him that he means something when he means nothing. But there is a curious interest even in the spectacle of an unpractised thinker wrestling with the technical language of modern thought. The philosopher may learn from it something of the dangers to which he also is subject. He may ask himself whether he too is not liable to think that he means more than he does mean ; and he may make a resolve never to use an abstract term until he is sure that he cannot express himself in concrete terms. But perhaps, if the correspondents of the silly season found that they were playing the part of drunken helots, they would cease to write to the newspapers at all.

HOLIDAYS NEW AND OLD

THE first Monday in August is a holiday, not only of modern origin, but peculiarly modern in its character. Its very name shows that it has no associations and is not connected with any person or event. It is a holiday made by Parliament ; and if we still think of the word holiday as keeping any part of its old meaning, it is not a holiday at all, for there is no special holiness about it. The day was chosen because it comes at a convenient time of year. No one could object to it for that reason. It is better that we should have law-made holidays than none at all ; but the fact that it was made in this way and that for forty years it has kept its cumbrous Parliamentary title is characteristic of our modern way of making holiday and of doing many other things. We have in the last hundred years, sometimes deliberately but usually through the mere force of events, cut ourselves off more and more

Modern Essays

from the associations of the past, and so from one of
the chief natural sources of wholesome and common
pleasure.

The old religious holidays, because of their connection with the Church, were holidays for everyone, and
their religious origin suggested the pleasures and sports
proper to them. The modern Bank Holiday is mainly
a holiday for one class, and its pleasures usually have
no connection with its origin, even when its origin
is religious. Everyone, no doubt, is glad to see the
people enjoying themselves on a Bank Holiday, and
efforts are made everywhere to organise amusements
for them. But every kind of amusement has to be
made; it has not grown; and it is devoid of the
romance and the traditions which draw all classes
together, not merely to amuse themselves, but to
celebrate some festival in a manner worthy of its
significance.

The August Bank Holiday, at least, has no significance except that it brings a day's cessation from toil;
and there is no reason why those who do not need a
rest should celebrate it. Therefore they do not celebrate it, and it is not a festival at all, but merely a day
of rest or pleasure for the poor. There is, of course,
an elaborate organisation for the purpose of amusing
them; but their amusements are in the main passive;
they buy them with their money rather than make
them themselves. They are audience or spectators,
rather than actors, in them. And the reason is that
these amusements are, for the most part, new and
peculiar to their class. It is easy to provide them with

235

something to look at, or to convey them somewhere in excursion trains; but they have to a great extent lost the power of amusing themselves because the well-to-do, who ought to be their leaders in amusement, have lost the same power.

We have all of us specialised too much in our pleasures, and disconnected them from the rest of our lives. We associate pleasure with idleness, not with happy activities; and the result is that, having lost the power of co-operation in our pleasures, our classes are estranged from each other by sharp differences of taste. There is no class now that habitually makes its own music; but some like to listen to good music and some to bad, and so there is no possibility of enjoyment common to both. It is incomprehensible to the cultivated rich that the uncultivated poor should like gramophones and " cinematoscopes " and crude melodramas. But the cultivated rich are cultivated usually only because they can pay for good entertainments, not because they can entertain themselves. Their cultivation has no effect upon the poor because it is not diffused by co-operation in any common amusement. It is passive, and therefore barren.

These are gloomy thoughts for a holiday, but the mere fact that we are now so keenly aware of a great defect in our modern life is hopeful. That defect became prevalent because no one was aware of it. Puritanis taught the English people to despise amusements; and as a result we lost the power of amusing ourselves, but not the desire to be amused.

Many reasons have been given for the decay of

236

music in England; but the real reason was that the English people came to think that music, being a source of pleasure, was not worthy of their serious attention. They were ready to buy it from foreigners, but not to make it themselves. Now we know that it is worthy of our serious attention; and in consequence we are becoming once again a musical people with wonderful rapidity. The proof of this is to be found, not in the operas and concerts listened to by the rich, but in the choirs of the poor. These and their achievements prove that bad taste is not a natural and inevitable result of poverty, but is produced by a desire for art which can get no proper satisfaction. Directly the poor learn to sing for themselves, they learn to like good music, as they liked it in the past. Music is only one of many pleasures that they have to learn afresh; but it is the best of all for bringing classes together in a common enjoyment, as our ancestors knew. Everyone who can sing can belong to a choir, and, if it is a good one, everyone who cannot sing can listen to it with pleasure. Every year our Bank Holidays are becoming more and more musical festivals; and therefore we may hope that in time they will be festivals for all classes alike, and that the rich will look forward to them as much as the poor.

GOOD FRIDAY

THERE are some commemorative days of the Church which should obliterate all differences of creed, because the observance of them turns our minds towards truths which we all need to remember, but which we are apt, among the absorbing trifles of our daily life, to forget. One of these is Christmas Day, the day of common rejoicing; another is Good Friday, the day sacred to unworldliness, the day of common mourning for the worst error the world has ever committed. It commemorates the extreme of defeat and ignominy and pain, and in doing so reminds us of that doctrine which, threatened by the passing heresies peculiar to each successive age, has been handed down from generation to generation of saints and heroes; the doctrine that success in this world is not the test of life, and that only when men despise it are they most divine and free from the slavery of material things.

It is easy enough to give a general assent to that doctrine, but most difficult to make conduct and judgment conform to it in any particular case. For the worldly success which the saints and heroes despise is not only the vulgar success of wealth and power. They have a purpose and a standard which make them indifferent to the moral judgment of the world; they have a constancy which is not shaken even when they are condemned as evil-doers by the appointed judges of the people. The Crucifixion is so far away from

238

us now that we are often apt to think only of its
symbolical side, to regard it, indeed, as an event
almost as purely symbolical as the Cross which commemorates it. The Cross is everywhere, and has
changed from a symbol of shame to a symbol of glory.
Therefore, it seems to us that the Scribes and Pharisees
who contrived the Crucifixion, and the Jewish mob
who applauded it, were guilty of a unique perversity.
That was the common opinion of the Middle Ages,
when the Jews were despised and persecuted for the
enormous sin of their ancestors. But we have to consider whether we, by any peculiar moral discernment
or courage, can prove that in the same circumstances
we should not have acted with the Scribes and Pharisees
or shouted with the mob.

That the Crucifixion is symbolical is, indeed, pro-
foundly true ; and the lapse of ages has not made its
symbolism obsolete, even for those who are not Chris-
tians. The Cross, once a symbol of shame and now a
symbol of glory, proves how easy it is for the world to
reverse its judgment after the event, but how difficult is right judgment at the moment. We have to
remember that the world, which in this case triumphed
in an error and an iniquity so terrrible, was not that
world which vague preachers of righteousness are apt
to denounce. It consisted, not of profligates and
idlers, but of all that seemed most respectable. It
was not merely brute force that won that evil victory,
but learning and law and order and religion. This
world, no doubt, saw in its triumph a proof of its own
righteousness. There never was a victory that seemed

more complete, or a vanquished cause that seemed more utterly lost. Nothing remained to it but a few obscure fugitives, so despised that no one thought it worth while to hunt them down ; and the boldest of these denied his Master.

No one, whatever his religious belief, disputes these facts, or the subsequent triumph of the Cross. Therefore, even apart from religious dogma, the Cross should be for all men the symbol of a faith at least in the doctrine of saints and heroes, which is questioned and threatened now as much as it ever has been. We find it difficult to understand the perversity of the Jews, because their heresies are not ours ; for heresies change with the fashions of men's thoughts, whereas the true faith is everlasting, and its truth is more easily seen at a distance than close at hand. Men die for it, like Socrates, and their death is remembered when the errors that caused it have lost their charm. The world is always unworldly in its judgment of the past.

Worldliness itself can applaud unworldliness when it has won its certain eventual success. The difficulty is to recognise its glory in the moment of failure, and to rise superior to the worldly heresies of the moment. For these, since they are always peculiarly fitted to the circumstances of the moment, have the glitter of novelty while those circumstances last, and are superseded by more glittering novelties before they are refuted. Our peculiar worldliness is not the worldliness of the last generation. We pride ourselves on our freedom from the hypocritical and sentimental errors of our fathers ; but our modern worship of the

Strong Man is an old heresy condemned by a poet long
ago ; and his words, translated by another poet,
sound as new as the heresy which they condemn :

> " O Strength of God, slow art thou and still,
>   Yet failest never.
> On them that worship the ruthless Will,
> On them that dream, doth His judgment wait,
> Dreams of the proud man, making great
>   And greater ever,
> Things which are not of God."

That worship of the ruthless will is only the worship
of success disguised with a new philosophical or scientific jargon.   When Euripides denounced it there was
no long tradition or experience of the true faith to
support him, nor was there any universal symbol of
it to which he could appeal.   All the ages that have
passed since he wrote the *Bacchae* have at least achieved
this, that we have the Cross to warn us against every
new form of the worship of success, and the recurrence
of Good Friday to remind us that what was once the
symbol of shame to all the world is now its chief
symbol of glory.

HASTE AND WASTE

BRIGHT skies and dry east winds in June produce a
deceptive appearance of perfect summer weather.
Both in the fields and in the garden the flowers which
normally mark the progress of summer by slow and
regular stages succeed one another with a hurried
intensity which simulates productiveness.   Summer

hastens on, as though in its richest uxuriance; but, if we look a little more closely into the vegetation and blossom of the time, we see that its apparent vigour is fallacious. The bright, dry weather which hastens the maturity of the year's plants has an equal effect in restricting their growth and in shortening the period of their bloom. A country walk in almost any district of England shows how fine, dry weather can be bought too dearly. The cool but thirsty east wind has licked the moisture deep out of the soil, and has annulled in a very few days the effect of each rare fall of rain. Hay crops are short and thin, oats are already in ear and will furnish little straw, and in many districts the scanty grass in the pastures puts a stronger temptation upon farmers to yield to the short-sighted policy of selling their young stock for food. Kindred blights fostered by the drought have fretted the June blossom and verdure which at first sight seems so vigorous and forward. In hedge after hedge almost every young green shoot is seen to be crumpled and fretted by the small but multitudinous insect pests which flourish when there is a lack of regular showers to destroy them. The wild roses, which are the very crown of the year's blossom in the fields and thickets, have been so thickly attacked that on many rose-bushes there are very few perfect flowers. The wild rose stands as the type of the fresh luxuriance of the earlier English summer, before the season of flowers changes to the graver time of harvest ; and its pierced and tattered petals sum up the blemish of a droughty year.

The secret of prolonged and fertile growth is in the

Modern Essays

grey wet days which make spring and early summer superficially unkindly and depressing. The richest crops come from a long preparation under warm and rainy skies ; the promise of a wet May and dripping June is well known to farmers.

A kindred principle rules the formation of human character and the efforts of human societies. We do not know with what feelings, if any, the young flowers and corn of May regard the grey and dropping skies of a wet spring ; but we know that the development of human character is benefited by times of preparation and restraint like those which the grey skies bring to the corn, and that they are wont to seem dull and gloomy. Anxious to begin its task, human nature in youth is impatient to end growth quickly, and eager for the forcing winds of maturity, which are as welcome to it as the clear sky. Nature produces the richest crops in the fields when the green growth is latest prolonged and the flower is slow in forming; and the fullest products of human character come from a long training under temperate restraint. This is the true human economy ; and by the use of foresight and intelligence we have the power of securing this period of deliberate training for almost any need or emergency. The corn and the wild roses have no such power. They are filled or pinched by the season according as the wind may blow ; and the hasty and impeded productiveness of nature after a season of sunshine and drought is an image of reproach to a nation faced with the waste of life that is the consequence of its want of preparation.

Modern Essays

VISIONS OF NIGHT

MIDSUMMER nights in northern latitudes change the
normal earth known to waking man into a kingdom
of mystery and the imagination. All night long, in
fine weather, the northern quarter of the sky, that is
normally the seat of darkness, is transfused by the
unsleeping sun ; and often the pale light that joins
day to day is intensified into a clear green or yellow
glow that emerges into the rose of morning. The
normal illumination of the moon and stars is dimin-
ished ; the diffused and lingering light of the sun
seldom gives them their free and accustomed scope ;
their lights seem to have dissolved and fallen to earth,
where the elder-blossoms loom by the thicket and the
meadowsweet begins to gleam by the rivers. Nearly
up to Midsummer Day the nightingales still sing ; and
their song gains a haunting mystery at night which
is not apparent in their vigorous melody by day,
when comparatively few people recognise it. Song-
thrushes sing late into the luminous dusk, while black-
birds fling out a few sweet strains before morning ; and
both their songs rival the nightingale's in power and
beauty, and are often mistaken for it in regions where
nightingales do not sing. The silence of the midsummer night is as haunting as its music. As layer after
layer of quiet is stripped away by the listening ear, it
detects a fresh stir of subtle and distant sounds, until
the earth seems full of reverberations as old as Time.

Modern Essays

The spirit grows enlarged with the immensity of its perceptions, and awed by the horizons that begin to open beyond its daylight powers. The glow in the north that stands upon the Arctic confines of undimmed brightness seems to shine also on the verge of that kingdom of the spirit from which all inspirations come. At last the treetops shiver, the air grows cool, and with the passage of the wind of dawn the light in the north takes on the clear colours of morning.

We cannot see clearly by the northern glow, for all its luminous brightness. Just as our eyes need daylight to fulfil their function, the right medium of our mental activity is the world as we see and feel it after the wind of morning has passed, and not the strange nocturnal earth before it. The physical exhilaration that follows the wave of fresh air is an index of the mental return to the conditions with which the mind is framed to grapple ; and very often, after we have watched in unwearied wonder the brief but solemn passage of a midsummer night, the immediate effect of the change is to make us long for our natural sleep, like children after a late party. It may appear irksome and humiliating that summer after summer we are accustomed to spend in inert and sense-less slumbers the hours of this wonderful nocturnal display, when the illumination of the sky seems to spread into the depths of the spirit, and our under-standing is enlarged as our hearing catches the bark of farm-dogs on hills leagues distant and the stir of filmy insects about the grass. But the spectacle of the midsummer night is very much to us what the late hours and lights and music of the party stand for to the children—something which delights the mind and kindles the imagination, which is stimulating on exceptional occasions but is not conducive to steady health and growth. In mind, as in body, we are normally diurnal creatures. Our powers can be trained and directed most consistently by the perceptions and judgments of broad daylight, and not by the visions and revelations of night.

THE SEASIDE

THAT the seaside is a great institution every one will readily admit, but everyone does not realise how much it means. It has established itself so naturally and gradually as the national playground and health resort that we take it for granted and forget that there was a time—not so very long ago—when people did not go to the sea for their holidays. As a general resort it is the child of the railway, one of a large family and not the least valuable, though seldom taken into account in reckoning national assets.

Sea-bathing seems to have been first appreciated by the doctors in the second half of the eighteenth century, when Brighton and Weymouth, under Royal patronage, began to supersede inland resorts. In the days of the post-chaise and the stage-coach such delights were only for the wealthy or those who lived within easy reach; but it is a noteworthy fact—unrecognised by sociologists—that, whenever anything comes to be regarded as beneficial, efforts are soon made to diffuse its benefits; and in 1792 a bathing establishment for poor patients from London was erected at Margate. The introduction of the steamboat brought Margate within easier reach of London and rapidly increased its popularity. Elsewhere the same process went on, where opportunity offered. Thus the ground was prepared, and when the railroad came it found the world eager to be taken to the sea.

The development since then has been continuous, and its effects have permeated the whole population. It has been greatly fostered by the gradually increasing attention paid to the welfare of children, which is one of the most interesting features of our time. The discovery was made that, if the seaside is good for adults, it is an incomparable place for children. That is the great advantage which it has over all other resorts. Mountains are no good for children; inland waters are dangerous for them; in the fields they are destructive; golf links know them not; and as for those places where people go to work off eleven months of unwholesome habits by a month's violent revulsion called a cure, children happily have no lot or part in this insane proceeding. There is no place for them like the seaside if they are to go anywhere. On the shore they are safe, healthy, and supremely happy; and as the custom of going somewhere in the summer became general the imperative interests of the children made every good mother long for the sea. It came to be the great family resort, and one section of society followed another.

As a popular institution the seaside is a great set-off to the urban life to which an ever-increasing proportion of the population is condemned in all industrial countries; and it is one which we, who suffer more from that condition than any other people, are able to enjoy more fully and generally than any other. No populous and industrial country has a coast-line so extended, so varied, and so accessible as this teeming little island. None needs it so much, and it is what used to be called a dispensation of Providence that we should have it.

The phrase is old-fashioned, but it would be hard to find a better, for surely if anything deserves to be called a blessing this does. Here is the antidote to our dreadful urban congestion brought more and more within reach of all. We make great use of it already, though we might, and doubtless shall, make more use of it as time goes on. It is a factor in the national life which students of social and economic conditions overlook, perhaps because it owes nothing to legislation or agitation and cannot be reduced to statistics.

The family exodus of the comparatively well-to-do for a month or so is only part of it. The extension and improvement of travelling facilities have brought about two developments. At one end of the scale the nearer seaside places have become regular suburbs to the large business towns in their neighbourhood. London is, of course, the great example. Its suburbs now stretch all along the coasts of Kent and Sussex, not to say Essex, Suffolk, and Norfolk, in a chain of towns, large and small. New ones are constantly springing up, while old ones grow and become more residential. The same process is going on in connection with other large towns not too far from the sea, such as Liverpool, Bristol, Cardiff, Hull, and Norwich.

But the other development is more interesting as a sign of the times, and that is the increasing enjoyment of the seaside brought within reach of the poorer classes. It goes on all round the coast, and no inland town is too remote to share it. For Londoners the two most popular points are probably Yarmouth and Southend, though Margate, Brighton, and other places get a large share. Nobody who has not seen the East-end disporting itself at Yarmouth knows what London is. But Lancashire beats London. There the great cotton towns disgorge practically the whole of their inhabitants upon the beaches of Blackpool and Southport, and that not for a day's outing only, but for a full week, for which the operatives save up during the year. The Yorkshire mill folk descend on Scarborough, Filey, and Cleethorpes ; the artisans of the Birmingham district and the bootmakers of Northamptonshire have farther to go, but a wider choice, and the railways make little of distance. The excursions to the seaside go on in all directions for weeks, and the cost is almost nominal.

The accessibility of our sea-coast makes this possible, and that is its greatest, though not its only, advantage. All our neighbours have adopted the seaside as an institution, but as yet only for the well-to-do. France, the favoured land, has most things that are desirable,

and a magnificent sea-coast is one of them. It is of
great extent and as varied as our own; indeed, more
varied in one respect, because it is washed by the
Mediterranean as well as by the Channel and the
Atlantic, and the Mediterranean gives it winter resorts
which we cannot rival. But it is all far too remote
for the industrial and even the lower middle classes in
the large inland centres of population. In France the
seaside is as yet a fashionable and expensive institution.

To the Germans it is still more inaccessible. Their
own resorts on the North Sea have peculiar attractions,
and are now, with the rapidly growing wealth of the
country, enormously frequented, but only by the well-
to-do. For industrial Germany the seaside does not
exist. They have their excursions on the Rhine and
the Elbe, to the forests and the hills, and to many
pleasant places; but the sea-air and the salt water
are not for them.

Belgium and Holland have developed their seaside
resorts in an astonishing way within recent years,
but these are for the most part cosmopolitan, fashionable, and gay, though some smaller and quieter ones
may be found. Portugal has a delightful coast, never
far from the railway, and bathing is a great institution
in the month of September. There is a string of
pleasant little bathing towns all along the coast; but
there, too, the sea is a fashionable amusement. Nor
is it otherwise in the United States. We alone have
made it a popular thing and a general boon shared by
all.

Modern Essays

THE COMING OF SPRING

In February the worst of the winter may be still before us, but every warm day that comes persuades us that it is spring. Even if there is no sun, the rainy west winds, that in December were only playing with the litter of autumn, seem now to be shaking the earth out of its sleep. Whatever flowers there are in the garden are no longer belated, but prophetic. They are not the sodden blossoms of untimely roses, but aconites, snowdrops ; even a crocus here and there in the sun, or an adventurous primrose. They are all adventurous rather than desponding, like the first light of dawn rather than the last of sunset. And in sheltered places among the hills there is new growth—not only catkins that have their own absurd spring when it is still autumn for everything else, but dog's mercury and the little new leaves of the honeysuckle, and all kinds of annual weeds, goose grass and cranesbills, which are busy growing wherever they get the chance. And the blossom is swelling on the elms and beginning to show its silver furry tips on the willows ; and on the banks of the swollen streams the golden saxifrage is already giving a promise of blossom.

ndeed, there is nothing like a little valley stream for persuading one that spring has come in February. It runs as busy and full as if it were fed with melting snows from the mountains ; and it makes one believe that it is the voice of a mountain spring, that wonder-

ful sudden spring in which all the waters are unchained
in a day and the flowers open as the snows upon them
turn to streaming shallows in the sun.

Our spring does not come like that in one triumphant
rush and glitter and chorus. It promises and disappoints, it advances and retreats; but still we feel
the difference between its earliest promise and the last
belated day of autumn; and the birds feel the difference too, and talk of it in a different voice, more
eagerly and busily, as if they were warned by the change
in the sunlight and the stir of the wind that their
time of work and happiness is coming.

One wonders how early the swallows in their southern
winter quarters begin to grow restless, and when the
cuckoo remembers the English woods of last May and
feels that his African forest is growing stale and dull.
For these happy wanderers there is no news except
of the change of the seasons, and they do not know
that men in their folly and pride believe that at this
moment they are determining the future of the world.
For them the world is only the earth with its natural
future and changes; and, though thay have to wage
the struggle for life, they have made no religion of
it. It comes, and there may be at any moment a
spasm of terror and death; but it is not foreseen or
glorified or painfully prepared for. They have no
souls perhaps; but, having none, they do not misuse
them; and we can understand why Christ spoke of
them and the lilies of the field to men for whom the
soul had become only a thorn in the flesh and a rankling
trouble to itself.

Modern Essays

We cannot, like them, live without theories; but, in our superior wisdom, what theories we make for ourselves; what nonsense we tell each other, as if we were gods watching the spectacle of the universe and reporting upon it, when all the while our theories are only disguised instincts and evil humours and appetites mistaking the way of their own satisfaction. Think of the Germans when spring comes, and how all their learning and industry have made them slaves, toiling without joy in their filthy trenches, and with no purpose but destruction. And we, too, have to toil against them so that they shall not ruin the world and make it all joyless and purposeless and German. But our men at least keep their fun and their sense of the absurdity of it all. They are not like a swarm of ants fighting with the deadly seriousness of instinct. They know that they have something better to do, if only their enemies would let them do it. They can laugh at their own duties while they perform them, and at the whole spectacle of a life in which men have made these duties necessary.

Laughter, they know, is the gift that man has given himself in compensation for his own failures. It may be bitter, but it keeps him above an animalism without the freedom and joy of animals. He may make a hell for himself; but so long as he can laugh at it he knows that in making it he is not fulfilling his destiny. He sees the incongruity between what he is and what he might be; and so our men in the trenches will see the incongruity between their business and the joy of spring; and they will make their jokes about it, hiding their desire for freedom and peace because they know that they can have neither until those unlaughing enemies of theirs have learnt either to think rightly or not to think at all.

THE TEMPERANCE OF SPRING

WITH the flowering of the hawthorn bushes the tide of the year's blossom reaches its full height. Not even the wild roses and the elder bloom, which soon follow, strew the land with blossom in such shining masses; and after the elders have faded, the ebbing of the tide of blossom becomes much more marked. It is typical of the coolness and freshness which underlie all the luxuriance of nature in England that the blossom which marks the climax of vegetative energy is so nearly white. Hawthorn blossom has not the absolute whiteness of the plum and cherry bloom, which covers many landscapes a few weeks before it. The extreme purity of these earlier blossoms is no longer in harmony with the wealth of verdure in maturer spring; and every hawthorn flower when fresh is tinged in the centre with delicate green, while the petals have the whiteness of milk rather than of snow.

At first sight this subtle accommodation of the hawthorn blossom to the luxuriant greenness of the landscapes among which it blooms may appear a solitary accident; but the more closely we examine the splendid

profusion of flower and blossom in the late May landscapes, the more we see that all their predominant
colours are merged into a harmony in which freshness
and not mere brilliance is supreme. A railway
embankment covered with blossoming broom, or a
riverside pasture shining from end to end with buttercups, seems at first sight to blaze with sheer gold.
But when we look at the blossoms in relation to their
surroundings, we see that the golden buttercups
harmonise rather than contrast with the luxuriant
greenness of the spring grass ; and where an oak tree
hangs its young foliage in the sunlight above the
brake of broom, its green leaves are hardly less yellow
than the yellowest of all May flowers. The leaves
and grass of May are almost yellow, and its yellow
flowers are so full of the freshness of spring growth
that they seem to melt into the verdure. The green
and the gold are alike so fresh and tender that they
harmonise with the dominant hawthorn blossom,
which is so subtly tinged to match them that its general
effect in the May landscape is still snow-white.

The association of such fresh and tender colours
with the crown and heyday of the year has a powerful
though often unsuspected mental influence. Much as
we overlook the delicacy of the luxuriant spring colours
until we analyse them, we do not realise their effect
on our mental standards until we compare them with
the hues of other seasons. If the intenser colours of
some later flowers were equally common in May, and
as widely distributed as the buttercups or hawthorn
blossom, either the spring would pall upon us, for

Modern Essays

very satiety of splendour, or the love of it would not
equally dwell in our minds as a love for what is fresh
and clean.

Barely a month after the hawthorn blossom marks
the height of spring the cornfields begin to be tinged
with the vivid scarlet of the poppies—the only scarlet
wild flower of our restrained English flora, with the
doubtful exception of the red pimpernel. Weeds
though they are among the corn, a field of poppies
makes a splendid display of colour, and leaves its own
pleasurable memories ; yet, if their colour left the pale
of the summer cornfield and ran riot over the brakes
and hedges in spring, it would rob spring of much of
its sweetness.

Still more tropical and feverish would be the effect
of some giant purple heather blooming in spring above
the lanes and pastures, although heather has its own
great beauty, sometimes intense and sometimes
autumnally drowsy, on open moors and wastes when
the year is declining. Colours have potent associations,
deeply drawn from man's physical constitution and
surroundings ; and the fresh flowers and verdure of
our springtime help to implant in no trifling degree
those mental standards of restraint and moderation
which we transgress at our peril.

Modern Essays

BEAUTY AND DESTRUCTION

As spring glides into summer, there is a peculiar beauty
and attraction in the young green foliage that fledges
an ancient and shattered oak. The year's new verdure makes a contrast with the splintered and silvered
limbs on which it springs like that of each generation
of youthful life among the buildings of an ancient
school or university. The gnarled bark and channelled
heart-wood of an old stag-headed oak have an aspect
of lichened stonework rather than of live timber
among the verdure of a park or pasture at this time;
and the freshness of the young foliage is enhanced by
the scarped and rocky limbs on which it springs.
When we see the bare pinnacles of a ruined oak up-
lifted above the round green crowns of the elms and
beeches, we may be apt at first to ascribe its characteristic impressiveness to the fact that it is a ruin.
But there is not the same attraction in other trees
when they fall into decay. A split and cankered
ash gives an impression, not of majesty, but of disease;
and when we occasionally find an ancient beech,
shedding sheets of bark carved with dates more than
a century ago, its aspect is more pitiable than vener
able. The attraction of an ancient oak is due, not to
its lifeless boughs, but to the tenacity with which it
still fosters its annual life; its significance lies, not in
its decay, but in its vitality.

If beauty lay in ruinousness, the destruction wrought

by war would be as admirable as it is actually hateful. There is only a difference of degree between the devastation inflicted in France and Flanders on cathedrals and town halls and mellow farms and the slow fret of time or human negligence. In days when we are being made familiar with the ruin inflicted by war, we should gain a clearer perception of the essential morbidity of the taste for ruinousness. If Tintern or Furness Abbey in decay is more attractive architecturally to any section of taste than either building would have been in the days of its perfection, then the same taste must logically accept the Cathedral of Reims or the Cloth Hall at Ypres as embellished by the German attacks. The ruin of our own ancient monuments is, from the purely æsthetic point of view, only more tolerable than that of the recent injury to the great buildings of Champagne and Flanders because we have had so many generations in which to get used to it. The ivy and other parasitic growths which still drape many old buildings are slowly continuing the destruction of the architecture that they hide; and the admiration which this kind of decoration sometimes excites is a tribute not to the building, but to the processes which are annihilating it.

On the old oak its native verdure is beautiful because it is a mark of vitality; but intrusive shrubs on an old building are instruments of destruction which ought to be tolerated no more. Because many people have never realised the essential connection between vitality and true beauty, they believe that usefulness must generally be content to be unsightly, and find as the corollary of this notion, a kind of beauty in what is physically sickly or structurally decayed. The beauty of Reims or of our own ruined abbey churches sprang as closely from the builders' concentration on what they most definitely held to be a practical object as the leaves of the oak from its sap; and the most modest modern building can be made at least seemly if the architect can accept its utilitarian object without impatience, and develop his artistic design, not as a compromise with utilitarianism, but as its expression. When the strong potentiality of beauty in whatever promotes active human life is once recognised, mere sickliness loses its charm; while the vital spirit which often burns in a frail body retains the pre-eminent attraction of the fresh foliage brightening the ancient oak.

MAN AND NATURE

EVEN into orderly and cultivated English landscapes the fulness of spring brings something strange and alien from human life. The hayfields that looked so drab in winter, and will become so tame again in July after the crop is mown and carried, are now densely springing jungles of animal and vegetable life, set apart from the world of human traffic by their white frame of wild cow-parsley under the hedgerows. The hedges are material obstacles raised by man, but the screen of white May flowers erects a barrier which is intangible and spiritual. It is impossible to enter such a

close of May verdure and pause in its stillness without
being conscious either of a readjustment of the mind
to the calmness and security of the green shade under
the white blossom or—as is more likely in times of
anxiety and stress—of the alienation of the mind from
such peace.   Unable to share fully the natural sweetness of the spot, the mind is apt to turn for refuge to
its material and man-made aspects.   We dwell in the
hayfield, not on the spontaneous and varied vigour
which Nature displays in this first harvest more than
in any that come later, but on the fertile promise of
the crop.

But we cannot roam far among the byways of
England in high spring without coming to many
gardens of Nature in which man and his material
interests have no share.   Broken cliffs lift to the sun
inaccessible gardens of sea-pinks and bluebells, sometimes only a few yards distant for the eye, but un-
trodden by any human foot.   Quagmires in sloping
woods, where the whole earth bulges in precarious
fatness, are rich with marigold blossom and shooting
iris, among which no heavier creature passes than the
long-toed waterhen.   Fishermen pressing up rocky
streams in the soft May evenings pass under veils of
alder and ivy to still more secluded gardens on the
hanging rock, where light mosses and lobed liverworts
make a dewy background for pale clusters of anemones
and primroses, and vivid tufts of wood-sorrel with
its delicate bells.   Man has no part in the maturing of
these lonelier gardens ; the flowers and mosses of the
rock are absolutely independent of his efforts, and are

seldom even looked upon by his eyes. They linger in the midst of our crowded island with an acute and inevitable challenge to our accustomed ways of thought.

Conscious of the beauty of wild flowers and verdure, and traditionally assuming that they are created to give us pleasure, we are apt to regard such lonely and isolated gardens as lacking something of their fulfilment, and as suspiciously like a flaw in Nature's design. The flower " born to blush unseen " is taken by the poet as an illustration of restricted opportunity. To those who know the perfection of the loneliest wild gardens, where no modification introduced by man has disturbed the pristine vigour of the natural society, the flower unseen is the flower unmenaced and unviolated. When we are brought face to face with the serene and secluded beauty of these wild gardens, the question aroused in us is not so much why they exist as why we do. Beside their perfection, the deficiencies of our own unsatisfied natures are emphasized. The superiority of the confused and agonising human life over that of the flowers in the green shrine moated by the stream assuredly lies in no achieved perfection, but in the possession of a will to resolve and plan and moral consciousness which makes perfection always inaccessible and disaster an ever-present contingency. Because our life is better than that of the flowers on the rock, it can become unspeakably worse. The serene and soulless natural world is incapable of the degradation to which the possession of an active intellect and a positive will can lead us if the dictates

of morality become obscured; and the wild gardens
warn us to take care lest the qualities by which we
excel in nature become its greatest profanation.

HORSE-CHESTNUT BUDS

WITH unfailing spontaneity and perfection, the large
buds of the horse-chestnut trees unfold in April complex tufts of rayed leaves and spikes of undeveloped
blossom. The expansion of these delicate clusters is
one of the most beautiful features of spring even in
country gardens; but their vigour and delicacy are
enhanced by the sooty and barren surroundings which
they annually transfigure in London. Unlike the
planes, which cast off large scales of smoky bark and
face autumn in dappled cleanliness, the smooth trunks
and boughs of London horse-chestnut trees are darkened with a grimy wash at all times of year. No tree
seems a more unlikely parent of the delicate tufts
which brighten April in London; and though the
budding of the horse-chestnuts is as familiar a feature
of the London calendar as the chant of the lavender-
seller in late July, or the first sound of the muffin-
man's bell in autumn, it recurs every year with the
same sense of almost incredulous surprise.

If human life were longer, we might in time grow
so used to the apparent miracle of spring's return that
it gave us little pleasure; but although time flies
quicker in later life than it does in childhood, when

the wonder of spring's transformation is greatest, a
year remains a sufficiently large fraction of our whole
experience for spring to keep for us until the end a
great measure of its earliest fascination. If certain
aspects of nature reappear in a fixed cycle at all, the
cycle appears to be too vast for one human lifetime.
There are spring days of brilliant colour and clearness,
showery lights in piled summer skies, and gorgeous
autumn sunsets which we remember once but watch
for in vain again ; and we realise, as time goes on,
that many manifestations of our climate may only
appear once in a lifetime, while others may be still
rarer. Our lives are set to a scale in which the recurrence of spring is frequent enough to gather many
associations, yet rare enough to keep us still children
at heart when it recurs. Beneath the young sprays
of the horse-chestnut trees in London parks and
squares we regain each April the wonder which is the
incentive to all knowledge, and the vitality which is
stored in a child's mind.

The leaves and flower-buds of the horse-chestnut
are packed and folded in their cases with the precision
of the most delicate human handicraft ; yet the more
we look at them the stronger appears the difference
between human craftsmanship and their natural
growth. We do not merely feel that, although the
form of the leaves, the down in which they are com-
pressed, and the sticky scales which enclose them,
might all be reproduced by a Japanese workman so
cunningly as to deceive the eye, yet no hand can make
buds which expand day by day into the fuller cluster.

The most significant contrast is less obvious, and reflects less on our inability to originate life than on our methods of dealing with it. In order to produce one of the well-grown horse-chestnut trees now putting forth their buds, Nature has taken thirty or forty years over raising it from nut to seedling and on to its mature period of blossom. Even the buds of the present spring have been waiting in their sealed cases for six months since the old leaves dropped in October.

The same stream of life is in man; yet in dealing with human affairs we are apt to forget that the only way to produce the mature character which we desire is to cultivate it fitly from the beginning. We assume that a living fabric can be shaped to our liking at short notice by summary methods of craftsmanship, like those which we apply to material industries. But unless the desired character is already in men, and has been developed by a long train of circumstances till it is ready to burst its wrappings at a liberating touch, it is as hopeless to try to force them to assume it as it would be to try to produce horse-chestnut leaves apart from the tree. In neither case can the improvised imitation have life.

LIFE IN THE WIND

WHILE spring is still decked with few blossoms, the mealy bloom of the catkin-bearing trees begins to tinge their boughs with various colours against the

sky. Poplars with catkins in full blossom are pow-
dered with roan, alders with a pale and duller red, and
hazel-bushes at a distance seem dusted with greenish
yellow. Bees and the slight flies that visit the other
flowers of early spring neglect the obscure yet profuse
blossoms of these catkin-bearing trees ; the trees are
not dependent on their precise and curious ministra-
tions, but are mated blindfold by the wind. For some
weeks past the minute but brilliant crimson blossoms
of the hazel have been outthrust from the centre of
the still unexpanded buds, ready to catch the floating
dust of the ripe catkins when the spring wind shakes
it free in a sunny noon. The blunt female blossoms of
the alder and the poplars' long catkins appear later ;
and the male yew-flowers will soon shed their yellow
dust more thickly in a sudden gust than any of the
others, though these little blossoms, half-hidden in
the evergreen leaves, do not tinge the whole tree, like
the catkins of the hazel or poplar.

Each spring these wind-mated blossoms testify to
the largeness of nature's alternatives and the general
absence in her works of rigorous conformity to a single
rule. Side by side with flowers of more flower-like
pattern their catkins preserve the profuse and hap-
hazard system of fertilisation by the wind. If the
evolution of plants had been accomplished under
human guidance, and a school or party of thought
had invented the method of fertilisation by insects,
or even self-fertilisation by contact of different parts
of the same flower, it would hardly have rested until
it had suppressed the system of fertilisation by the

wind as reactionary and unintelligent. Yet we do not find that the catkin-bearing trees fare any the worse for their method of managing their affairs. The hazel which conceives in the wind flourishes as heartily as the sallow in which the bees will soon be humming among the yellow palm-blossom ; and to the eye and mind of man nature is the richer for this variety. It is half an hour's liberal education first to discover among the hazels on a bankside the small crimson stars, of which the very existence is unsuspected by many country-dwellers, to mark how the ripe pollen smokes through the air at a tap of a catkin-laden bough, and then to watch the bees passing from bush to bush of blossoming sallow with their air of almost human precision. For all their accurate industry in the performance of their own work, the bees are ministering to an entirely different process of nature, of which they have no conception. Mankind is proud of the bee-like ingenuity and accuracy with which it pursues many of its activities ; but we cannot be sure that the main result of our labour is not something as remote and unsuspected by ourselves as its service to the spring flowers is by the bee. We do not always foresee the reactions of our most careful enterprises ; and, while the bee working among the spring blossoms may recommend us modesty, the wind calls us to hope. Not all that is blind and primeval is unprofitable and reactionary, any more than the skill of the human intellect tends always to credit and peace. When the March winds raging in the boughs of Europe have gone down, they may be found to have been pregnant with union and fertility, as well as winged with destruction ; and if we are to catch the seed of growth, we must keep an open heart as well as an intelligent purpose.

LENT LILIES

THE green spears of the daffodils, or Lent lilies, are strongly thrusting in gardens and hillside copses, and many are on the point of breaking apart to let drop their golden blossom to the sunshine. With the strong spring growth of their united stems and leaves, and later with the brilliant golden trumpet of their hovering blossoms, the Lent lilies seem conspicuously out of touch with Lent, although a perfect expression of spring. Though Lent means spring, the spirit of Lent and spring are very different ; and while it is easy to see the fitness of the association of Easter with the full growth of nature after the equinox, it is less plain at first why the earlier season of steady increase and promise should be held appropriate for special abstinence or discipline. This year to many persons who watch the return of spring the justness of this association must be plainer than usual. A discipline lies upon us, almost in our own despite ; and, if we think a little of the cause, we shall see why in all years the spring of nature is rightly the Lent of man, whether he conforms to Church observances or not. We cannot share in the full gladness of spring this year, because our attention is concentrated on a great struggle of human wills, which are outside the field where the lilies bloom. Though the fighting of the sparrows about their nesting-places is not more purely an appeal to force than our own means of settling our differences, the conviction on which our force rests is not equally dependent on the measured course of nature. We fight in spring, when a combative current runs in the veins of the birds; but we also tore each other in autumn, when most birds kept peaceful company in flocks and the air was full of softness and decline. Whether we are bent on upbuilding or destroying, on furthering a cause by peaceful intercourse or the sword, we draw our faith from the crucible of our inner consciousness, not from the winds and the sun; and this realisation of our human aloofness from nature will show us why even in kindly years we need to keep Lent in spring.

Man is in large measure freed by his mental powers from the obedience to a settled order of times and seasons which usually controls the natural world. In all kinds of ways we have a power over nature which beasts, birds, and flowers have not. It is this partial but all-important emancipation from natural law which distinguishes us from other animals, and makes us human in any sense worth the name. This freedom from natural restrictions gives us a far greater capacity for excess than exists in the purely natural order. We can almost disregard the seasons, and pursue our designs or desires unbrokenly from spring to spring. But it is a primary condition of our being that, while we are freed from the compulsory moderation which waxing summer will impose on the singing of the lark and the flowering of the daffodil, we are not immune from the consequences of excess. If we give free rein to any purely natural faculty which we share with the quarrelsome sparrow, even if our aggression is on an imperial scale and is organised in the name of intellectual pre-eminence, we are likely to perish of our excess. We prove and sustain our humanity by conscious dissociation from nature as much when the world is teeming and growing as when it wanes and darkens to mid-winter. But for deliberate restraint, our emancipation from nature's automatic control would prevent us in any year from enjoying the beauties of springtime itself with that sense of inner calm in which we seem not only to see but to share them. Fully to enjoy the Lent lilies, we must come to them with the spirit of Lent.

ON COLOUR

At the height of spring, and in autumn when the leaves are turning, every one notices colour and takes delight in it. But those who care for it most are most aware that the word falls short of expressing what they feel. They dislike the phrase " a beautiful bit of colour," because it seems to make a dull abstraction of what is concrete and glorious, because they know that beauty of colour cannot be separated from other qualities that make any object or scene beautiful.

The very blue of the sky, formless and intangible, is really an infinite distance of light. You may think of it as colour, and a painter may be forced to represent it by a coat of blue paint; but this word blue, separating colour from all other qualities, is merely a label attached to it by the mind, and by one part of the mind alone.

The sky, as a reality reaching the mind through the eye, is light as well as colour, and infinite distance besides; and it needs no science to tell us that it is not merely colour, or that the glory of it is made by light and infinite distance. But as it is with the blue sky, so it is with all objects and phenomena that delight us with their colour. The spring gentian on the mountain-side is blue also; but it is a little star exquisitely shaped so that in it the blue seems to be an expression of its eager but straitly confined life; and, where there are thousands of these stars in the short mountain turf still wet with the melted snow, what delights us is the multiplicity of this eager life, as if there were a choir of clear voices singing altogether a song that no one had taught them. Their blueness, indeed, is not mere colour to us, but a quality of their being, and no more to be thought of separately than the quality of sound in Mozart's music.

Indeed, in all flowers colour is nothing without form, even when we see them at a distance or in millions. Poppies in corn are not a smear of scarlet, though a dull painter may paint them so and satisfy a dull spectator. However thick they be, their colour has a life and stir and meaning in it given to it by the shape of each single flower, the endless variety and repetition of it, and the manner in which it takes the light and shadow with its curves. To see only colour in this is like hearing only sound in poetry. In both cases the meaning, and with it the actual delicacies of colour and sound, is missed. For the eye cannot fully see, nor the ear hear, without the help of the mind ; and that is why people see, and painters paint, so differently. The pure sense of sight may be equal in two men, but in one of them the thing seen may stir no activity of the mind, in the other it may stir an activity that gives a further eagerness and comprehension to the eye.

If you look at poppies in corn expecting to see only a smear of colour, they will remain that and nothing more to you, and you will be quite content to use the phrase " a fine bit of colour." But if the poppy is a beautiful living thing to you, your mind will help your eyes to see all its life and beauty ten thousand times repeated ; nor need it persuade you that you see what is not there. This quickening of the eye by the mind will not show you ten thousand separate poppies each as distinct as if there were only one. It will only bring mere dead colour to life for you, making it like a choir to the eye ; with the meaning and diversity of form in it, which belong to it as much as the meaning and diversity of voices belong to a mass of choral sound.

Language, with its useful abstractions, is always a danger to us, pampering the purely intellectual part of our minds and persuading us that our senses tell us

less than they do tell us. And so our common use of
the word colour, leading us to separate it in our minds
from form, often does actually make us see less than
we might see. It is useful to distinguish colour from
form for intellectual purposes; but if the eye also
makes that distinction, it merely fails to see one or
the other of them, and is blind to an essential quality
of the reality.

It may be well enough to speak of bluebells as a
mist of blue under the trees, because in so speaking
you wish to insist upon one particular quality of them.
But if you see them only as a mist of blue, you might
as well be looking at the smoke of your own cigar in
the train. Bluebells, however innumerable and however far seen, are still bluebells; and there is the character of their form in their colour, even though it
glimmers for you in the dusky distance of a wood.
And cherry blossom, though you see it like a bloom
of light upon a far western hill, is still cherry blossom,
and would not look so if it were anything else. And
in all the colour of the woods, now flushing brighter
day by day, there is implied the structure of the
branches and the form of all the growing leaves; implied to the eye as well as to the mind, unless the eye
is dulled by the mind's abstractions and persuaded
that it sees what is merely an intellectual concept.
Now indeed is the time for us to quicken our minds with
our senses, when the sound means the bird and the
colour means the flower and the leaf as full of the
delight of spring as the words of poetry are full of their
meaning.

Modern Essays

"NATURE"

FOR the poets Nature has always been feminine, and
spelt with a capital like any other proper name; yet
it is very difficult to discover from them who she is.
Sometimes, especially in the eighteenth century, she is
merely not Art; and in that case she is usually held
up to us as Art's superior. Indeed Pope and his school
speak of her with great respect, perhaps because they
had only a very distant acquaintance with her. But
then came the " return to Nature "; and when the
poets had returned to her they did not seem to know
whether they liked her or not. At first they felt that
she had done a great deal for them, and they wanted
to be in harmony with her. But Matthew Arnold told
them roundly that that was not possible or even desirable. He said that Nature was cruel, stubborn, and
fickle—" Nature and man can never be fast friends "—
to which Tennyson added that she was red in tooth
and claw.

By this time she was evidently not merely the opposite of Art. Indeed the more she came to be ill-spoken
of, the more did man begin to find himself included in
her, if not in harmony with her. The contrast between
him and his works and her and her works was becoming
less sharp; when he wished to excuse some weakness
of his own, he said it was only human nature, as if
Nature must bear the responsibility for whatever part
of her was mixed up with his humanity. Then came

the materialists, who said that the whole of man was Nature, since Nature was everything. For them, therefore, the word could not mean any one thing in opposition to any other. Indeed it meant too much to have any useful meaning whatever ; and yet it was a favourite word of theirs and one which led them into strange confusions of thought.

So strong was Nature's old feminine charm that they could not use the word without personifying the thing, although for them there was no thing, not even an abstraction, to personify. They would contrast man and his illusions with Nature and her realities, although, on their own showing, every illusion of man was just as much a part of Nature as a mirage in the desert. They advised man to study Nature, when it was impossible, according to them, to study anything else ; in fact, they went on opposing him to Nature just as the theologians had opposed him to God.

But this new opposition of theirs was not fair to man ; for, while he lost his place in a hierarchy of the Universe where he was a little lower than the angels, while, in fact, he was deprived of his immortal soul with all its hopes and fears, he did not get the compensations enjoyed by the black-beetle or the cabbage. No one contrasts them with Nature to their disadvantage. They and all their mental processes are Nature ; but man, though just as much Nature as they are, must mortify himself by wishing that he had Nature's virtues, or reproach himself for violating her laws. Yet it is Nature in him that violates her own laws ; and, if she is to be personified at all, it is she that deserves to be reproved for it. But, of course, she

274

cannot violate her own laws, nor can man, being a part of her. Whatever happens is in accordance with her laws ; and man only persuades himself that he has violated them when some law operates in a manner unpleasant to himself. Even to speak of laws in this sense is to imply some personification of Nature, as if she enacted them like a King or a Parliament. Her laws are merely our observation of what we call cause and effect. Certain things happen when certain other things have happened ; and there is nothing impressive or majestic about that.

But there is something impressive and pathetic about this persistent personification of Nature in minds that should have outgrown all such weaknesses. They had driven her out with a pitchfork, yet she comes back as personal as ever in all the glory of her capital. An end has been made of every creed, and then, amid all the austerity of modern thought, the primitive myths begin to grow again, as wild flowers spring up in an empty garden. They are expressed in a different language, abstract and unrhythmical, but the instinct is the same as that which imagined Aphrodite rising from the sea.

Nature, we are told, fulfils her own purposes heedless of our ideals, and punishes ruthlessly those who do not obey her. Well, all that has been much better said about Aphrodite, and with just as much truth. Hippolytus refused to love, and misfortune befell him. We neglect our drains, and misfortune befalls us. But there is no more purpose or punishment in one case than in the other. If we neglect our drain, bacilli flourish at our expense. It is a conflict in which

275

only we and the bacilli are concerned, and there is no
Nature to set the bacilli upon us any more than there
was an Aphrodite to inspire Phædra with a passion
for Hippolytus. Yet, just as temples were built to the
terrible and beautiful Aphrodite, so praises are sung
to this terrible and beautiful Nature, who defies all
our efforts to unthink her and who punishes them by
making nonsense of our thoughts. However hard we
may reason about it all, things outside us will not be the
same to us as we are to ourselves. They have a beauty
for us that we do not find in ourselves; and there is
something in us that adores it. We may not go so
far as the heathen in his blindness, who saw a nymph
amid the coolness and music made by a stream in its
hollow on the parched mountain-side, and for whom
the grapes created the God who gave them; but still
the spring and the mountains and the midsummer
moonlight go to our heads, and in the whispers of the
forest we seem to hear tell of a secret that everything
knows except ourselves. Then we call it Nature's
secret, and we are no wiser than the poets, except that
we refrain from making their songs; or than the poor
pagans, but that our foolishness does not betray itself
in myths.

A MORAL FROM BLACKBEETLES

A PARENT complained that his daughter, aged twelve,
a pupil at a secondary school, "appears to know all
there is to be known about the anatomy of blackbeetles and other vermin," but that, being asked the

names of the British Isles, she replied that they were
Europe, Asia, and Africa. The parent is indignant;
but there is a theory of education behind the child's
knowledge and ignorance. For blackbeetles are real
things to a child; she can see them living and moving
and having their very unpleasant being, perhaps, in
her own home; but the British Isles are too large to be
anything but mere abstractions to her. No doubt
she has been taught their names; but children, and
many grown-up people, have a great power of forget-
ting what they do not want to know; and the question, perhaps the most difficult of all questions in
education, is whether the child shall be taught what it
does want to know or what it does not. If you teach
it only what it does want to know, it will be, no doubt,
astonishingly ignorant in what is called general information, unless it happens to have a taste for it.
If questioned by an uncle it will put its parents and
teachers to shame; but, on the other hand, it will
learn what it does learn thoroughly and with understanding; and to do that is a great part of education.
The parent complains that what his daughter learns
is a mass of rubbish which can be of no use to her in
after life. But if she is learning what she wants to
know, the mere process will be of use to her; and we
have a way of making what we want to know useful
to us, just as we make what we do not want to know
useless. Besides, we are taught at school a vast deal
of general information merely because it is considered
that a properly instructed child ought to know it; and
often it is information that we should learn in due course
without ever being taught it. This little girl, for

instance, would know the names of the British Isles and certain other facts of geography when she was grown up, if she had never been to school at all ; and education does not benefit us much by teaching us such things before our time, unless they are taught as a basis for some more special and more interesting knowledge.

The question is, therefore, whether a teacher shall try to give a child such general information that no one will be put to shame when its uncle questions it, or whether he shall follow the child's inclination in his teaching ; and this question is made more difficult by the fact that many children show no inclination for any particular kind of knowledge. It is for these that the general information system has been devised. You must teach them something ; and, since they cannot tell you what they want to learn, you teach them the names and dates of the Kings of England, or even of Israel and Judah, or the journeys of St. Paul, or the length of the chief rivers of the world. And all this is supposed to be useful information because it is commonly taught. It might be useful, if the pupil made any use of it afterwards ; but he, and still more she, forgets it as soon as school is over. If this little girl marries and becomes the mother of a family, she will have no use for the date of the battle of Hastings, except to teach it to her children ; but what she learns about blackbeetles may help her to get rid of them. That is the crude, practical side of the matter ; and we put it to her parent because he wants education to be sensible and practical.

But there is the other side to be considered too.

There is the mind of the child. If his daughter has
a passion for the anatomy of blackbeetles, the father
is to be congratulated ; for it is a sacred passion, even
if blackbeetles are vermin. Would he weaken that
sacred passion for knowledge by forcing her to learn
facts of geography or history which she does not want
to learn, and which therefore seem to her mere foolishness ? If you teach a child against the grain, you can
put it in love with ignorance. If you teach it what
it wants to know, it may learn to love all knowledge,
and at any rate to respect even that knowledge which
it does not love. We ought to come from school feeling that knowledge is a high and sacred thing, and
more ashamed of pretension than of ignorance. But
if we are taught what we do not want to know, pretension is our safeguard against the attacks of our teachers,
and we come to regard it as our safeguard in after life
against all that experience might teach us. If education has that effect upon us, it serves neither God nor
Mammon, and we should be better without it, even if
we did not know the names of the British Isles.

THE ROD AND THE CHILD

WHAT is the real educational effect of the temperate
and reasonable use in schools of the cane, birch, tawse,
or other implement of corporal punishment ? Does
it, as some say, destroy the self-respect of the victim
who holds out his hand or is stretched across the
block ? Does it, as others maintain, assist bad boys

to rise on stepping-stones of their dead selves to
higher things ?　There is no more vexed educational
problem than this; and it is quite natural that it
should have been discussed, the other day, by the
assembled members of the National Union of Teachers.
Though they discussed it, however, they cannot be
said to have settled it, for the excellent reason that
their interest in it was, in the main, professional and
one-sided.　Their concern, that is to say, was not so
much with the boy's eventful benefit as with the
master's immediate convenience.

The former branch of the subject is the one of which
we hear most when the relations between the rod and
the child form the topic of newspaper controversy,
and all sorts and conditions of respectable persons
publicly (though, as a rule, anonymously) attribute
their respectability to the stripes which they endured
in youth, and the fortitude with which they learned to
endure them; but the other branch of the subject is
also worthy of consideration.　Can a teacher reasonably be expected to maintain discipline without the
implements of discipline ?　If he cannot, then ought
not the law to indemnify him against actions for
assault on the part of the parents of children whose
misconduct brings the implements into play ?

That is the shape in which the question seems to
have presented itself to the minds of the majority of
the elementary teachers, who asserted that assistant
masters, as well as headmasters, possessed a common
law right to inflict corporal punishment.　Their
primary desire, that is to say, was not so much to expel
the old Adam from the rising generation as to be

Modern Essays

allowed, as it were, to bear arms in their own defence against the turbulent. And that demand, thus supported, raises, of course, the further question : If a man is to be a schoolmaster at all, ought he not to be able to keep boys in order by the sheer force of superior personality ? If he cannot do that, is it not likely that, even though he does wield the cane, his class will still be disorderly ?

These are matters on which opinion seems, at present, to be in a state of transition. In the old days, immortalised by the educational achievements of Busby and Keate, those who had the reputation of being " strong men " were the men who caned most frequently and most severely ; but the stories which legend has handed down of the tricks played on them by the boys do not indicate that the rule of terror was a really efficient regime. Nowadays we are more inclined to ascribe the quality of strength to the man who makes a little caning go a long way, or even dispenses with it altogether—creating the atmosphere of terror, or at least of respect, without any overt act. There certainly are such men ; and they succeed in maintaining discipline in circumstances in which Keate and Busby would probably have been helpless—among those pupils of Army-crammers, for example, who are too old to be caned or punished in any other way, but not too old to make a weak tutor's life a burden to him by ingenious rowdiness.

It was among such that M. Jean Richepin, the French poet, once had experience as a teacher ; and he reduced the roaring lions to the quietude of lambs by the announcement that he had come amongst them

281

to earn his living, and that if any one of them thought he could prevent him from earning it he would settle the matter outside—*à coup de poings*—when the lecture was over. Other men are able to reduce similar anarchy to equal order without even the use of a threat, merely because the power to command and the confident expectation that obedience will be rendered is implied and conveyed by a vague something in their manner or their tone of voice. If all schoolmasters were disciplinarians of that stamp, the question of the cane would have little actuality or importance; and it is only because so many schoolmasters are not disciplinarians of that stamp that the question is so often and so hotly debated. Perhaps, as we require so many schoolmasters and pay them so little, it is too much to expect that they should all possess those exceptional gifts of presence and character; but it is nevertheless useful to remember, when we hear them clamouring for the cane, that the frequency with which they will use it is likely to be in inverse proportion to their effectiveness as teachers.

CHILDREN IN WAR-TIME

BEFORE the summer holidays of 1914 began, teachers no doubt set their pupils the customary holiday task. How many, we wonder, either of the teachers or of the pupils, have thought of those tasks again? The storm was threatening then, but it had not yet burst; and we are never fully aware of a storm while it is only a

bank of dark clouds in the distance, however swiftly
and inevitably it may be towering up into the nearer
sky. It is only when the sudden ominous wind begins
to blow and the first sharp crash of thunder sounds
and the first heavy drops fall that we know for certain
it is upon us. But these storms of nature we have
seen before. Not even the oldest of us has ever known
a storm like this, made by the folly and panic and
irrational pride of man, foretold and premeditated for
many years, but never realised in its action or its
consequences, and least of all by those who have
brought it upon us.

This, too, is a storm in which the labours of men
are not suspended, but rather intensified. One knows
how an ants' nest is quickened into activity by the
prod of a stick ; and all the declarations of war were
like a series of prods from the stick of some curious,
yet indifferent, giant. Each belligerent country was
swarming at once with its defenders and attackers
and all their subsidiary helpers, so that our imaginary
giant might have smiled at their furious but insignificant energy. And yet with all these new tasks of
destruction set to every nation by the blind folly of a
few, the old customary tasks have still to be carried
on. Nowhere, not even in Germany, can the nation
really be a nation in arms. Those who fight are,
economically, idlers or worse ; and they have to be
fed by those who are not fighting and who also have
to feed themselves. Not for a moment can mankind
stand idle and watch the spectacle of carnage they are
making for themselves. Even in the apprehension and
excitement of the first onset there is no suspension of

duty for anyone, but rather a heavier burden of it.
And the first duty upon all who are not soldiers, upon
young and old alike, is to remember this, and never for
a moment to allow their minds to be demoralised by the
thought that in this towering calamity of war nothing
matters but the war itself.

The word Armageddon has been very freely used
about this war; and, like all figurative and exciting
words, it has a misleading power. It is not Armageddon, because mankind will have a history after it
and because it is a war which men have made for
themselves and will have to end for themselves, and
after it is over they will have to go on living and
working as they lived and worked before it. There
are millions of children in Europe to whom some day
it will only be a memory; and the memory, we hope,
of something that will seem impossible in their own
happier time, of an experience and a lesson so sharp
that it need never be repeated. All these children,
with the future in their minds now so unknowing and
in their hands now so weak, have been entrusted to us
by the Power that gives will and conscience to our
flesh and with them gives to each of us His own share
in making the future of the universe. All these children now have their holiday; and what a holiday it
is that the world is making for them. In Belgium—
we dare not think of it; in France; in Russia; and
in the country of our enemies, where the children are
as guiltless as our own and where the war means only
the loss of a father, the silent, half-understood anxiety
of a mother, the sense that their own play and work
alike matter no longer, and that everything in their

life is threatened by some secret their elders will not tell them.

And, indeed, we elders have all of us together a secret that we cannot tell our children, a guilt upon our civilisation that we are only fully aware of when we look at them, for they alone have no part in it. We have inherited from the past, and some of our European nations have cherished and glorified, these instincts of the beast that make war still possible ; and for these children have to suffer with the rest of us ; and many of them will suffer long after the war is done. But we cannot tell the children this, and we would not, if we could, trouble them with our own fear.

Yet we can teach them to have a hope greater than our own ; even at this moment, and most of all at this moment, we can remember that the aim of teaching is to make the pupil, not like the teacher, but better ; for it is only with that aim that the teacher becomes humble and forgets himself, as an artist forgets himself in the glory of his art. We would not have the children learn, in this holiday of theirs, what we are doing with the world that our forefathers have handed down to us. But we can teach them to make a better world of that which we shall hand on to them. This time, we may be sure, will stay sharp and clear in their memories ; we can ensure that they shall have a wise and fruitful memory of it.

We know how our ancestors used to frighten their children with tales and threats of " Boney," which were only a grotesque shadow of their own fears, and it would be easy for us to teach our children the same primitive hatred and fear of our enemies. There is some excuse for us, perhaps, when we feel it, but there would be none at all if we taught it. We ourselves are in the present, and subject to all its shocks and emergencies. The worst part of us is always lying in wait for us, always encouraged by its counterpart in others. But we should know that it is the worst part of us; and we should no more wish our children to catch it than we should wish them to catch a physical disease.

For us the world as it is, and we must make what we can of it; but for them the future, and may that be connected with our present only by the best and not by the worst that is in us. Let us therefore be frank with our children to this extent, that we do not glorify to them the present bloody failure of our society. Let us tell them that we have failed, and not make a bogey of our enemies to bear all the blame. The blame is mainly theirs, no doubt; but for our children the German children will be the Germans, and there is no guilt on them. The future will be with the children of all nations, and it must not be poisoned by a vendetta from our generation. That is the holiday task that we can teach, and it is one that can free this sad holiday from the darkness of despair.

LEARNERS AND TEACHERS

THERE are some people who enjoy learning and some who enjoy teaching; but unfortunately—and this is one of the chief difficulties of education—those who enjoy teaching do not commonly enjoy learning. That is why many people do not care for the society of schoolmasters. They have a habit of teaching, and no one can complain of that since it is the habit of their profession ; but it often seems to have closed their minds against the habit of learning. And the worst of it is that the habit of teaching may be much more mechanical than the habit of learning ; indeed it always becomes mechanical when it is not combined with learning. There are schoolmasters, like the beaver that would build a dam on the desert of Sahara, who will go on teaching when nobody wants them to teach, and when they had much better be learning.

For you cannot be teaching all the time ; at least, if you are, you only repeat your teaching, which is as bad for the mind as to repeat your learning ; and when a schoolmaster repeats his teaching on those who have long left school, we may be sure that he is, as they say, functioning blindly like the persistent beaver. His business in the schoolroom is to know ; and there he has to adopt a schoolroom convention according to which there is nothing intermediate between knowledge and ignorance, between truth and error. But outside the schoolroom his business, like that of everyone else, is to learn ; and, if he is to do that, he must put away the schoolroom convention and remember that he only knows for the purpose of teaching, that in the world he himself is a schoolboy like the rest of us. The universe confronts him in all its glorious uncertainty ; and he will never understand it if he thinks that he knows it already, as if it were only an irregular verb.

287

But those who have the habit of learning find it equally difficult to acquire the habit of teaching. For their very love of learning comes from their sense of the glorious uncertainty of the universe. They are on a voyage of discovery through life, and have no time to write books of travel about it. They will talk eagerly about the latest experiences of their minds, but only because they want to live those experiences over again, to make them clearer and more intense. In fact, while they talk they are teaching themselves and not others; and they will never, if they can help it, present anything that they know as certain knowledge.

So the born learner is seldom a born teacher; and if, by any chance, he is a schoolmaster, neither he himself, nor the other schoolmasters, nor even the boys, consider him a success. The boys like to be in his schoolroom, but he does seem to them to mean business, and, to the stupid ones at least, he seems to know very little. Other born teachers remember him afterwards as the man who encouraged them rather than thwarted them; but in a school there is a need of masters who will constrain as well as encourage; for the world, either of boys or of men, is not made up of born learners.

But it does happen sometimes that the born learner is also a born teacher; and, when he is that, he is born to be a schoolmaster. His delight then is not only in learning himself, but in communicating his own surprise and delight of learning to others. He goes out into the world, and returns to his schoolroom like a bee laden with honey returning to his hive.

And the very contagion of his delight makes even
stupid boys understand what learning really is; that
it is a kind of experience, and not merely an exercise,
of the mind. And to this born schoolmaster teaching
itself is not merely a profession, but as much a delightful and surprising experience as learning. When he
teaches, something new happens to himself and to
his pupils. His own experience of learning is com-
municated to them as a poet communicates his own
experience of love. It is not that they know facts
which they did not know before, but that their minds
are growing like his and that he sees them growing,
as if he were a gardener making his own spring for his
plants. And to him the stupid are only difficult plants
that he never despairs of. To learn the secret of their
stupidity is for him a delight like another kind of
learning, and to teach them is an experience that never
becomes a routine.

SCHOOLMASTERS OLD AND NEW

THE pedagogue of classical Greece was a slave, and
there are those who hold that his position has not
greatly changed with the lapse of time. The παιδαγωγός,
however, was not a schoolmaster at all; and sensitive
teachers who detect a suggestion of contempt in the
modern use of the word may console themselves with
the thought that the pedagogue's duties are now divided
between the school-matron and the commissionaire.

Modern Essays

The repute in which the schoolmaster is held to-day
is probably higher than in any period of history;
for the development of language, which affords most
valuable evidence on all points of social precedence,
throws a singularly suggestive light on our ancestors'
view of the profession. Any good historical dictionary
will show the changes of meaning undergone by such
words as " sophist " and " usher." Admittedly, it is
always the majority who attach new shades of meaning
to words whose full connotation they may not understand; and schoolmasters, under whatever name,
have always been a small and not particularly powerful
minority. Such considerations are not very con-
clusive; and we should prefer to admit that, until the
importance of education as the basis of national
success was first understood in quite modern times,
teachers as a class exposed themselves rather freely
to the gibes and sneers which they clearly received in
full measure. Rightly or wrongly, men were believed
to teach not so much for the love of teaching as for
the somewhat frugal portion of loaves and fishes with
which teaching was rewarded. The profession passed
through many vicissitudes before it was seen that
national prosperity depended very largely on the skill
of the teacher; but when once this was fully understood, the teacher received a measure of respect
hitherto withheld.

The status of commerce has had a not dissimilar
history; in days when the position of a country
depended wholly on its prowess in war, men who sold
things for profit, on whatever scale, were almost as far

outside the pale as were the slaves of ancient Greece.
Socially they were ignored rather than despised.
To-day, when the economic strands can scarcely be
disentangled from the fabric of high politics, the man
of commerce is almost the social equal of the soldier,
provided that his dealings are on such a scale that
they may be presumed to be reflected in the trade
returns. As soon, therefore, as the makers of our
social standards are persuaded that a fellow-country-
man, be he tradesman or schoolmaster, is not wholly
impelled by motives of self-interest, social barriers
are removed from his path and the inflection of contempt from his style and description.

We need not pause to consider how far the makers
of our social standards are just and candid with themselves in attributing the altruistic motive to the captains
and not to the rank and file of the class with which,
purely for purposes of illustration, we have compared
the teaching profession. It is sufficient to note that
the altruistic motive is now attributed both to the
autocratic headmaster and to the lineal descendant of
the " usher " ; and that the " eternal public," which
Emerson assures us is always right, is now content to
direct the shafts of its ridicule elsewhere. So far, so
good ; but the teaching profession, especially the rank
and file, is beginning to think that the next step
towards making right and justice to prevail is the
wider application of the truth that the labourer is
worthy of his hire. Truths of this kind are grasped
very slowly by the general public acting on its own
initiative ; and, if we may refer once more to the

commercial analogy, precedent seems to show clearly that united action is the most likely road to success. Some grades of the profession are fairly well paid; others, notably the staffs of many secondary schools, are so far underpaid that their position is discreditable to the parents, the managers, or the ratepayers, as the case may be. The tendency of the time and of enlightened opinion is undoubtedly in favour of a more equitable distribution of the pecuniary rewards of teaching. These rewards, however, must remain, in any future which we can foresee, comparatively small; and the repute of schoolmasters, which owes some of its present dignity to the respect which the plain man ever accords to the altruist, will remain untarnished while the ideal of so many continues to be *Non sibi sed patriae.* Lord Ormont's Aminta, it will be remembered, respected enthusiasms, but " she could not understand enthusiasm for the schoolmaster's career." Matthew Weyburn, however, who knew the meaning of patriotism, had no ambition for any higher title than " School and Schoolmaster."